ADVERTISING IN INDIA

ADVERTISING IN INDIA
Trends and Impact

Om Gupta

Publications

KALPAZ PUBLICATIONS

DELHI-110 052

Advertising in India: Trends and Impact

ISBN: 81-7835-308-3

Reprinted in 2012 in India by
Kalpaz Publications,
C-30, Satyawati Nagar, Delhi-110 052
E-mail: kalpaz@hotmail.com

Printed at: G. Print Process, Delhi

Contents

1. Advertising, History, Changing Face and Ethics 9
2. Scanning Advertisements 47
3. Advertising Media, Agency Impact 55
4. Sex in Advertising 73
5. Advertising and Potrayal of Women 125
6. Impact of Advertising on Rural India 137
7. Targeting the Consumer 153
8. Importance of Business Communication 187

Index 225

1

Advertising, History, Changing Face and Ethics

The History of Advertising

Advertising is dated back to the Christian Era. One of the first known methods of advertising was outdoor signs, they would be painted on the wall of a building and were usually very eye catching. Archaeologists have found signs in the ruins of ancient Rome and Pompeii.

Advertising as we know it today began during the last quarter of the nineteenth century. If an advertising agent working on the account of a product such as Quaker Oats cereal in about 1900 were to have been transported forward in time to 1925, the challenges, choices, and risks he faced would have been in many respects familiar. If the same agent had been transported backward to 1875, that could not be said. Advertising agencies were relatively unknown then, and those that existed had ill-defined responsibilities. The mix of products for which they were placing advertisements was quite different from that on the market at the turn of the century Quaker Oats itself had not yet been invented. Thus, the history of advertising in America falls into two eras separated at about this turning point.

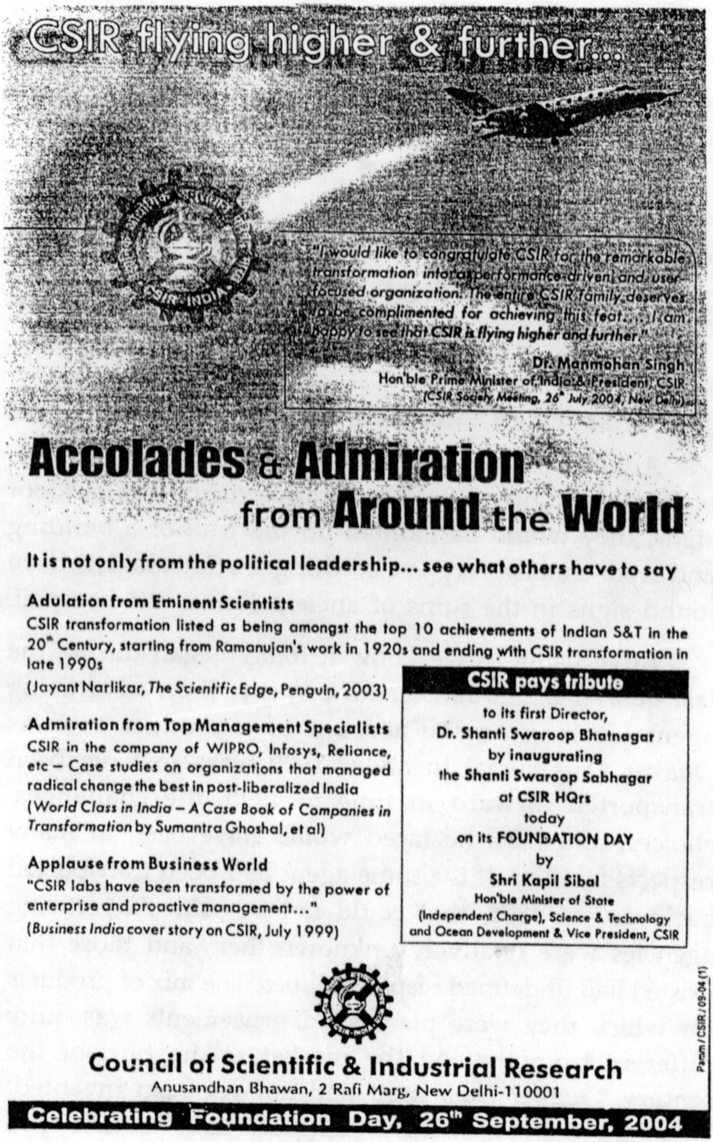
CSIR flying higher & further...
"I would like to congratulate CSIR for the remarkable transformation into a performance-driven and user focused organization. The entire CSIR family deserves to be complimented for achieving this feat.... I am happy to see that CSIR is flying higher and further."
Dr. Manmohan Singh
Hon'ble Prime Minister of India & President, CSIR
(CSIR Society Meeting, 26th July 2004, New Delhi)
Accolades & Admiration from Around the World
It is not only from the political leadership... see what others have to say
Adulation from Eminent Scientists
CSIR transformation listed as being amongst the top 10 achievements of Indian S&T in the 20th Century, starting from Ramanujan's work in 1920s and ending with CSIR transformation in late 1990s
(Jayant Narlikar, The Scientific Edge, Penguin, 2003)
Admiration from Top Management Specialists
CSIR in the company of WIPRO, Infosys, Reliance, etc – Case studies on organizations that managed radical change the best in post-liberalized India
(World Class in India – A Case Book of Companies in Transformation by Sumantra Ghoshal, et al)
Applause from Business World
"CSIR labs have been transformed by the power of enterprise and proactive management..."
(Business India cover story on CSIR, July 1999)
CSIR pays tribute
to its first Director,
Dr. Shanti Swaroop Bhatnagar
by inaugurating
the Shanti Swaroop Sabhagar
at CSIR HQrs
today
on its FOUNDATION DAY
by
Shri Kapil Sibal
Hon'ble Minister of State
(Independent Charge), Science & Technology and Ocean Development & Vice President, CSIR
CSIR INDIA
Council of Scientific & Industrial Research
Anusandhan Bhawan, 2 Rafi Marg, New Delhi-110001
Celebrating Foundation Day, 26th September, 2004
Panm / CSIR / 09-04 (1)

Sydney Central City
TRIGGER
1932 JEANS INC
NO ESCAPE
IS THE KEY. CAUTION FROM HORMONES, THAT CAN GO BERSERK ANYWHERE, ANYTIME. EXPERIENCE IT WITH THE LATEST COLLECTION FROM TRIGGER THAT'S STYLED AT THE 1932 JEANS INC STUDIO.
WATCH OUT! YOU NEVER KNOW WHO'S ON THE PROWL.

To begin with, we should define advertising. It is mass communication an advertiser pays for in order to convince a certain segment of the public to adopt ideas or take actions of benefit to the advertiser. During the past century, large American manufacturers have played a leading role in developing this craft, but in earlier years, leadership in terms of design and creativity lay elsewhere.

In the eighteenth century, Great Britain boasted the most advanced advertising. Handbills and trade cards proclaiming in extravagant terms the excellence of sundry products and services were common. Among the items being sold, few if any caused more excitement than the New World itself. Signs and handbills touting its wonders were so ubiquitous in London that Richard Hofstadter has observed that America was conceived amidst "one of the first concerted and sustained advertising campaigns in the history of the modern world." Daniel J. Boorstin believes that such promotion may have had a significant impact on the speed of emigration and has wondered about the impact on American civilization of the fact that "there was a kind of natural selection here of those people who were willing to believe advertising."

Advertising was a well-established practice in the late colonial and early national periods in America, but these advertisements were neither as appealing to the eye nor as cleverly crafted as were their counterparts in England. The type was so illegible that Benjamin Franklin observed: "If you should ever have any secrets that you wish to be well kept, get them printed in the papers." Moreover, the United States was a predominantly rural nation. Its farmers may not have been totally self-sufficient, but they produced more of their own food, clothing, and household items than did urbanites. Thus, more Americans focused on production for survival than on consumption for pleasure. With a sparse, predominantly rural population and without an efficient system of transportation and communication, the country had neither the need for nor the means of concerted national advertising campaigns.

Most advertising during the early national and antebellum periods was repetitious and unimaginative. Writing of the pioneer merchants on the middle border, historian Lewis Atherton observed that "in general the early advertising was dreary, matter of fact reading, served a limited purpose, and was completely devoid of ... customer appeal... one advertisement was like all others." There were advances in American advertising in the larger cities during the 1820s and 1830s with improvements in printing technology and a change in advertising philosophy. James Gordon Bennett, Sr., New York Herald and other New York penny press newspapers prided themselves on speaking directly to the mass public in understandable and accessible terms, and they wanted their advertising to have the same appeal. In 1848, Bennett began changing the Herald's advertisements every day, making them news just like the editorial matter. The precursors of advertising agencies also date from this period. By the 1840s, Volney B. Palmer was listing his "coal and advertising" agency in New York City's business directory. The very description of the business–coal and advertising–illustrates how undifferentiated advertising was in those days.

Modern advertising really began in the 1880s, when new methods of manufacturing led to greatly increased output and decreased costs for the producers of consumer goods. Advances in packaging technology meant that products could be packaged at the plant rather than shipped to a wholesaler who traditionally broke bulk and put his own name on them. Moreover, the telegraph network was in place and the continent had been criss-crossed by a network of railroads, bringing its farthest reaches within the purview of the incipient consumer culture.

Prior to the 1880s, the American marketing system had been characterized by an intricate set of wholesalers, jobbers, and other middlemen whose most important function was to buy in large lots and sell in smaller ones. In this age, the wholesaler was king. But in the new era of the 1880s, the importance of the packaged goods manufacturer greatly increased. What manufacturers could package at their own plant, they could brand. What they could brand, they could advertise. What they could distribute nationally, they could advertise nationally. Daniel A. Pope has written, "This necessitated the growth of advertising agencies and dictated their activities" and also "tipped the balance in advertising from information (however specious much of it had been) to persuasion."

National advertisers provided the media and advertising agencies with a new set of clients whose standards of conduct were far higher than those preceding them. The most widely advertised consumer products through most of the nineteenth century had been patent medicines—nostrums for which their purveyors made extravagantly false claims. But the new companies, although not always innocent of misstatements, depended upon repeat-purchase behaviour and thus upon building a bond of trust with the consumer. To do this, they had to eschew blatant falsehoods.

As late as 1893, according to Pope, more than half of a sample of over a hundred firms spending more than fifty thousand dollars annually on advertising were patent medicine manufacturers, whose advertisements were often of the "cancer cure" variety. His list of the largest national advertisers some twenty years later showed a sharp contrast. Most of these firms were not "medical messiahs" but manufacturers of food, consumer chemicals like soap and cosmetics, and consumer durables like automobiles and auto accessories.

For these new firms, advertising served many purposes: The management of the distribution system. Manufacturer advertising could pressure distributors into stocking products because advertising created consumer demand. A consumer might feel more loyalty to a heavily advertised brand like Coca-Cola than to a particular soda fountain and thus not patronize a fountain that did not carry Coca-Cola.

For the consumer product marketer, advertising became the marketing analogy to assembly-line production techniques. It was systematized mass salesmanship, which became a key weapon in the arsenal of companies seeking to create and build brands.

With the new mix of advertising clients and the new conception of advertising came a host of changes in the trade that sharply differentiated twentieth-century practice from the previous era. Among the most important changes were those in the areas of copywriting, research, and source of compensation.

Through most of the nineteenth century, the principal function of the nation's advertising agencies was to buy space in publications at wholesale and sell it to advertisers at retail. In 1892, the N.W. Ayer and Son agency in Philadelphia hired its first full-time copywriter to write the advertisement itself. Soon after, Albert Davis Lasker of the Chicago agency of Lord and Thomas greatly boosted the prestige of the copywriting function within the agency. He founded the "reason why" school, which held that an advertisement had to give the customer a specific reason (perhaps a more accurate description would be "rational-sounding excuse") to purchase a product. This approach contrasted with the bulk of previous copy, which had often consisted of an announcement accompanied by disconnected and incredible claims to excellence.

Modern business corporations and advertising agencies make a major effort to research the projected and actual impact of their advertising. Research at agencies dates back at least to 1879, when Ayer undertook its first such project. Since then agencies, their clients, and independent market research firms–often assisted by marketing academicians and economists–have spent large sums to determine advertising's effectiveness.

Advertising agencies have always been intermediaries between advertisers and the mass media. During much of the nineteenth century, it was unclear whom the agency represented. Was it primarily a seller of media space or a seller of a manufacturer's product? In the twentieth century, the answer has been the latter.

Agencies sell products by buying space or time and are compensated by manufacturers.

The most visible change in advertising in the past hundred years has resulted from the new technology of broadcasting. Initially, many thought that advertising over the "ether" would never be accepted by the public because it would constitute an obnoxious intrusion into the home of the owner of a radio set. And even if it did not prove unacceptable on grounds of taste, many felt that radio advertising should be prohibited as a matter of public policy. When he was secretary of commerce, Herbert Hoover said at a conference on radio in 1922 that it was inconceivable that we should allow so great a possibility for service to be drowned in advertising chatter. By the end of the decade, however, advertisers and their agents had come to realize radio's possibilities. With its drama and immediacy, radio could convey their message directly to the consumer who would not need to purchase a publication or even be literate.

In the 1950s came television, which was commercialized in the United States to an exceptional degree. American advertisers had more minutes to telecast more commercial messages to more market segments (including children) than anywhere else in the world. Through television, advertisers could demonstrate the use of their product and present well-known figures to praise it. As had been the case with radio, those companies that first exploited the commercial potential of television reaped lavish rewards.

Advertising–The Process

How advertising works requires a definition of what advertising is.

One definition of advertising is: "Advertising is the non-personal communication of information usually paid for and usually persuasive in nature about products, services or ideas by identified sponsors through the various media." Now let's take this statement apart and see what it means.

Non-personal

First, what is "non-personal"? There are two basic ways to sell anything: personally and non-personally. Personal selling requires the seller and the buyer to get together. There are advantages and disadvantages to this. The first advantage is time: the seller has time to discuss in detail everything about the product. The buyer has time to ask questions, get answers, and examine evidence for or against purchase.

Finally, the seller can easily locate potential buyers. If you enter a store, you probably have an interest in something that store sells. Street vendors and door-to-door sellers can simply shout at possibilities or knock at the door and start their spiel with an attention grabber. From there on they fit their message to the individual customer, taking all the time a customer is willing to give them.

Disadvantages do exist. Personal selling is, naturally enough, expensive, since it is labour-intensive and deals with only one buyer at a time. Just imagine trying to sell chewing gum or pens one-on-one; it would cost much more than a Rupee a stick or pen. In addition, its advantage of time is also a disadvantage.

Communication

Communication means not only speech or pictures, but also any way one person can pass information, ideas or feelings to another. Thus communication uses all of the senses: smell, touch, taste, sound and sight. Of the five, only two are really useful in advertising—sound and sight.

Introduction

Advertisement is a form of mass communication, a powerful marketing tool, a component of economic system, a means of financing the mass media, a social institution, an art form, an instrument of business management, a field of employment and a profession.

Advertisement means 'Public announcement'. It involves communication with the public about a product idea or service through a medium to which the public has access. The medium may be print (such as newspapers, magazines, posters, etc.), electronic (Television, radio, internet etc.) or any other.

An advertisement is a form of persuasive communication with the public. The communication is usually one-sided, in one direction from the advertiser to the public. The members of the public are free to respond to it in their own way the response is at an individual or family level. There is little or no dialogue with the public advertising forces itself upon the public. At the same time, especially in a democracy with a market economy, such communication is required so that intelligent choices are made.

Definition

The American Marketing Association, Chicago, defines advertising as: "Any paid form of non-personal presentation and promotion of ideas, goods and services by an identified sponsor".

Analysis of Each Element of this American Definition

Any form. Advertising may be in any form of presentation. It may be a sign, a symbol an illustration, an ad message in a magazine or newspaper, a commercial on the radio or on television, a circular dispatched through the mail or a pamphlet handed out at a street corner, a sketch or a message, on a billboard or a poster or a banner on the net. Any form of presentation, which an advertiser imagines will fulfill the requirements of an ad, can be employed.

Non-personal. This phrase excludes any form of personal selling, which is usually done on a person-to-person or on people-to-people basis. If it is a person-to-person presentation, it is not advertising.

Goods, services, ideas for action. It is well-known that advertisements are employed to communicate information about products and services. Advertising is necessary for companies to send out information about products that would cost customers too much to seek out on their own.

Most definitions neglect the use of advertising to promote ideas. The Posts and Telegraph department advertising to promote the us of PIN code for faster delivery of letters is an example of selling an idea for action. The Income-Tax Department advertising to persuade the income-tax payers to pay their taxes before the due date to avoid default is another case of the application of advertising to ideas involving action.

Openly paid for by an identified sponsor. This means that advertising is openly and directly paid for as against publicity, which is not openly paid for. As it is paid the sponsor has control over the form, content and scheduling of the ad. The sponsor too is identified. The company's name or brand name or both identify the sponsor. If in an ad, the sponsor is not identified and it is not paid for its use of the media in which it has appeared, then the message is considered to be publicity. The publicity material when prepared, may be paid by its sponsor, but the newspaper, magazine or radio station that carries it does so free of charge.

Advertising, A Form of Mass Communication

When a marketer or a firm has developed a product to satisfy market demand after thoroughly analyzing the market, there is a need for establishing contact with the target market to eventually sell the product, moreover, this has to be a mass contact which means that the marketer is interested in reaching a large number of people so that his product may receive optimum exposure. Naturally the best way to reach this mass market is through mass communication and advertising is one of the means of such mass communication along with such other means as publicity, sales promotion and public relations.

Advertising as a means of mass communication has, therefore, made mass selling possible. It is perhaps the best-known mass communication channel. Marketers and firms engaged in selling their products and services throughout the country and or in other nations are fully aware of the necessity and importance of advertising. As a means of forceful communication, advertising promotes the sale of goods, services, images and ideas through information and persuasion. But one thing may be well-understood advertising by itself cannot sell the product. It cannot sell products of poor quality, and products which are two costly, or items which do not come up to the expectations of the consuming public. Advertising only helps in selling

Advertising Benefits the Advertiser

- Advertising establishes a link between the manufacturer and the consumer. It is a form of mass communication. Through advertising, the advertiser reaches a vast number of consumers, and makes his product known to them.
- Advertising makes it possible for the manufacturer to introduce new ideas and new products.
- Advertising keeps the consumers well informed about the products and services-styles, features, sizes, colours, specifications, prices, availability, instructions for use etc.
- Advertising expands markets, builds up volumes, gives a market share and profitability, reduces prices.
- Advertising makes product adoption process smooth. It sells corporate ethos and builds up corporate identity.
- It is correct to say that advertising is a business as well as social process.

For a manufacturer, advertising conveys information to his customers, persuades his customer and reminder them about the product.

Advertising Benefits the Consumers

- Advertising has made its presence felt after the war years when buyers armed with the purchasing power had the capacity to buy but not the will to buy. Advertising created that well and converted into an effective demand.

- Advertising guides the consumers in his product choices. It gives the information about the product, benefits it offers, the availability and the price.
- Advertising makes us aware of many socially relevant causes like dowry, energy conservation, loss prevention, social forestry etc. Advertising is thus a friend, philosopher and guide of the consumer.
- Advertising at times describes a product, at times narrates a story or an experience, at times educates a consumer.
- It is a time saver for the consumers. It also gives the consumers promised performance, a promised quality. It gives cost benefits. It delivers standard of living.

Advertising contributes to consumer welfare. It helps consumers in a variety of ways. It tells what to buy, how to buy, where to buy and why to buy.

Types of Advertising

It is conceptually more interesting and analytically more important to classify advertising. The basis of classification, however, can be diverse. The principle means of classification are:-

(I) By geographical spread

(II) By target group.

(I) By Geographical Spread

On the basis of geographical spread, advertising can be classified as:

(a) *National advertising:* Some manufacturers may think that their target is the entire country. They select media with a countrywide base. Generally large, established firms belong to this category. Among them are Hindustan Lever, Brooke Bond. Larsen and Tubro, Escorts, Associated Cement companies and the like.

(b) *Local advertising:* Small firms may like to restrict their business to state or regional level. Some firms first localise their marketing efforts and once success has been achieved, they spread out to wider horizons. A classic example is Nirma Washing Powder, which initially was sold only in Gujarat and subsequently entered the other markets.

(c) *Global advertising:* Multinational firms treat the world as their market. Firms such as National, IBM or Sony or Ford advertise globally, e.g., in periodicals like *Times, Reader's Digest.*

(II) Target Group

On the basis of target group aimed at, advertising can be classified as:

(a) *Consumer advertising:* A very substantial portion of total advertising is directed to buyers of consumer products who purchase them either for their own use or for their household's. The fact that buyers of consumer items are generally very large and widely distributed over a large geographical area enhances the importance of advertising as a marketing tool. The preponderance of such advertising can be seen by looking into at random any general print media, such as newspapers and magazines etc. These advertisements are indented to promote sale of the advertised products by appealing directly to the buyers/consumers. Such advertising is called consumer advertising.

(b) ***Industrial advertising***: Industrial advertising on the other hand refers to those advertisements which are issued by the manufacturers/ distributors to the buyers of industrial products. The category would include machinery and equipment, industrial intermediates, parts and components etc. Because of unique characteristics of industrial buying decision process, the importance of industrial advertising is comparatively lower than that of consumer advertising.

(c) ***Trade advertising***: Advertisements which are directed by the manufactures to the distribution channel members, such as wholesalers or retailers, are called trade advertising. The objective of such advertising is to promote sales by motivating the distribution channel members to stock more or to attract new retail outlets.

(d) ***Professional advertising***: There are certain products for which the consumers themselves are not responsible for the buying choice. The classic examples are Pharmaceuticals where the decision is made by doctors while the consumer are the patients. Firms operating in such market segments, therefore, have to direct their advertising to these decision-makers, who are professional people. Such advertising is called professional advertising.

Advertising in India

In March 1980, the silver jubilee of the Advertising Club of Bombay (Mumbai) was celebrated. An audio-visual review workshop was arranged on 25 years of Indian advertising; and the dominant feeling at that time was one of self-congratulation with a certain amount of introspection. Indian advertising has grown to its maturity and become very professional. We have advertising clubs in each of the major metropolitan cities and have as many as about five hundred advertising agencies vying with each other in wooing large accounts. The advertising club of Bombay is the Mecca of Indian advertising, contributing about 60 per cent of the total billing of the advertising industry.

We have professional bodies, representing the three parties concerned with advertising, i.e., the advertiser, the advertising agency, and the media of advertising. The ISA–The Indian Society of Advertisers–is the sole representative body of advertisers. The AAAI–The Advertising Agencies Association of India represents agencies in the industry which undertake advertising on behalf of advertisers. The INS–the Indian Newspapers Society–is the organization of newspapers, magazines and other publications. Similarly broadcasting companies have organized under the banner of the Indian Broadcasting Society (IBS). Today the gross billing of the advertising business has increased from Rs. 10 crore in 1955 to about Rs. 160 crore in 1978 to Rs 8000 crore in 2000. This was possible because of the phenomenal growth of such media as television, radio and cinema in addition to the large number of new products introduced as a result of the industrialization and economic development of the country. Newspapers and magazines alone registered an impressive increase during the last ten years. Internet has enraged as a medium of the new millennium.

Indian advertising has yet to shed its elitist urban image and open up the vast rural market which in per capital terms may be poor but which in the aggregate is an important market segment (70 to 80 per cent of the Indian population resides in villages) to which advertising has not yet spread to the desired extent besides this, it has a great role to play in assisting in the eradication of poverty, for 46 per cent of our population lives below poverty line, in communicating the availability of goods, services and opportunities and in contributing to improvements in living standards.

Indian cultural diversity poses a huge communication challenge, but this should not be used as an excuse to play to the gallery.

Let us remember what Ghoshal, the former Chief Executive of HTA has to say about Indian advertising: Advertising is absolutely essential. Unless a product sells, the investment made in the project is senderad infructious. But the trouble with Indian advertising is that it is not rooted in our ethos. It is Westernised partly because most of our advertising is aimed at the urban consumer. But there should be a mix so that advertising can sell products and yet retain the Indian flavours Ghoshal also believes that advertising has improved tremendously over the last four decades in terms of technical excellence, particularly graphics and copy, but has not made much progress in terms of relating to the consumer. Good advertising is advertising that sells unfortunately most of our advertisements are made with a view to impress peers rather than the consumer.

There are specialised advertising agencies like Pressman Advertising and Marketing. It controls around 75 percent of the total financial advertising in the country. There are casting agencies who help the aspirants getting roles in films, or on TV or modeling assignments.

All this shows a growing professionalisation of Indian advertising and by large its future is bright, provided that those in the profession acknowledge the social responsibility of advertising and conduct themselves in such a way as to be seen as an important part of the economic development effort of the country.

Ten Memorable Ad Campaign in India

Product	*Campaign Theme*
Dalda	*Mamta ki kasauti par khara* Mother's who care
Liril	A luxurious bathing experiences
Air India	Maharaja
Surf	Bucket wash concept made acceptable
Terene	Creaseless and so no ironing required
Amul	Utterly Butterly delicious
Thums Up	Happy days are here again no missing on Cola
Maggie Noodles	Bus Do Minute
Onida	Neighbour's envy owner's pride
Hamara Bajaj	Social Mobility

Different Media Used in Advertising

In advertising terms, medium is a channel of communication such as newspapers, magazines, radio and TV. A medium is a vehicle for carrying the sales message of an advertiser to the prospects. It is indeed a vehicle by which advertisers convey their messages to a large group of prospects and thereby aid in closing the gap between producer at the one end and the customer at the other end. Different media are organizations or enterprises for entertainment. They sell the product in form of newspaper, magazine and radio and television programmes. At best, they are service organizations fulfilling the needs of listeners, readers and viewers for entertainment and information.

Types of Media

The media are classified into two categories:

I. **Above the line media**: The recognized agencies get commission from these media. Such as TV , radio, newspapers, magazines, internet, etc.

II. **Below the line media**: Those who do not give commission to the ad agency. The agency adds a percentage as a handling or profit charge or charge a service fee. The examples are: hoarding, banners, posters, direct mail, wall paintings, etc.

The following are the various categories of media available to an advertiser:

1. **Print Media**

   (i) Newspapers–Daily, weekly, Sunday, weekend supplements, etc.

   (ii) Magazines–Consumer magazines, business publication, etc.

   (iii) Direct advertising–Direct mail.

2 Broadcast Media

(i) Radio–Vividh Bharti, FM.

(ii) Television–Terrestrial Channels like DD and satellite channels like Star, Zee TV.

(iii) Narrow-cast media–Video and Cable TV, Cinema, Ad Films.

3. Other Media

(i) Speciality Media–T-shirts, buttons, caps, stickers, badges, etc.

(ii) Outdoor Media–Hoardings, posters, bus shelters, etc.

(iii) Internet–Media of the new millennium.

The media selection is done on the basis of reach of the medium, exposure time and some other factors. The reach of these medium is very good in urban areas. There are more than 12 crore newspapers copies daily, 15 crore radio sets, 9 crore TV sets, 1 crore computers, 51960 printed publications, 5638 dailies in all languages including 407 in English and 2507 in Hindi. There are 10000 cinemas, 1013 films with at least 50 lakhs spectators.

Hence, there is a solid reach to the masses. The people who live in cities are addict to all these mediums especially above the line mediums.

The History Channel

Paul W. Farns and John A. Quelch, Advertising and Promotion Management: A Manager's Guide to Theory and Practice (1983); Daniel A. Pope, The Making of Modern Advertising (1983); Richard S. Tedlow, New and Improved:

KNOW THE BEST SCOTCHES

The story of the smoother, milder and more appealing whiskey blend begins with a man who hailed from a humble background and rose to become one of the legendary Scotch whiskey barons of the 19th century. His name was James Buchanan. and he was driven by a desire to produce a superior brand that would attract a wider interest.

Although he realized that the market for Scotch whiskey was larger, Buchanan understood that it is an acquired taste; and that many people were dissuaded from imbibing the blends that were too strong in flavour. His intuition led him to anticipate that new blends of Scotch whiskey would have to be developed to meet the needs of potential consumers. Perhaps he also predicted that these blends would stimulate conversions.

Throughout the Highlands, Islands and Lowlands of Scotland, generations of distillers have used fresh barley, malted by fires of rich and aromatic peat. Distilled with the purest water drawn from Highland streams, each whiskey is matured for many years in specially selected oak casks until it has developed its full character and flavour. Many distinctive, single whiskies are produced in this manner, and these were the source of inspiration for the visionary who conceived the mellow blend over a century ago.

The components that make up the refined taste of this blend hark back to the long tradition of Scotch whiskey-making. The finest natural ingredients endowed by the Scottish landscape are transformed by the formidable skills of man into whiskies with an individual flavour. Handpicking only the finest malt and grain whiskies to achieve the delicate balance he was seeking between body and flavour, the pioneer created a unique concoction. Smoother and milder in character than other Scotch whiskies, it still retains the body and flavour that catapulted Scotch to the realms of renown. Even today, the master blender discerningly picks out each whiskey as it comes of age. and recreates the characteristics of the original blend that James Buchanan arrived at so many years ago.

Black&White
Unbelong
NIGHTS
COMING SOON TO YOUR CITY

Not everyone who wears a watch wants to know the time.

THE NAME GAME:
THE BIRTH OF A BRAND

Originally christened 'The Buchanan Blend' after James Buchanan, the new whiskey was sold in a black bottle with a white label. This characteristic brand packaging set it apart from its competitors and a growing number of customers began to ask for 'that black and white whiskey'. Bowing down to popular demand, Buchanan formally renamed his blend 'Black & White' in [illegible]. Two years later, in 1906, the name was registered as a trademark.

To celebrate the renaming of the brand, a series of advertisements were released in Punch magazine and other contemporary periodicals announcing that 'The popular Scotch whiskey is Black & White'. Buchanan was a great advocate of advertising and, being an ardent animal lover, he began to use motifs of animals in promotions for his blend.

The earliest were black and white illustrations of horses and dogs. But sometime during the 1890s, Buchanan returned from a dog show with an endearing photograph of three champion terriers, and so the seed was sown for one of the world's most famous trademarks. The image that grew out of this idea, featuring the black Scottish terrier and West Highland white terrier, captured the imagination of the brand's ardent admirers. And thus it came to be adopted as the brand's mascot.

1 November 2004 ■ OUTLOOK

good taste
fascinates
Seagram's
BLENDERS PRIDE
MAGICAL NIGHTS
Taste that speaks for itself

The Story of Mass Marketing in America (1990); Richard S. Tedlow

Ethics of Advertising

Advertising has been heavily criticized on a variety of counts. Economists have charged that advertising distorts competition by raising barriers to the entry of new firms into an industry and by distracting the consumer from price. Sociologists have complained that advertising barges into the home with pseudopopulist rhetoric ("We do it all for you") that in fact encourages a starkly materialistic approach to the world and promotes an ethos suggesting that what one possesses is more important than who one is. The historian of the content of advertising copy Roland Marchand has shown how advertisements adopt various clinches and parables whose relationship to a sensible evaluation of a product's benefits is tenuous at best. Indeed, much advertising copy conveys a message that, if not false, is not really true either.

Consumer advocates have accused advertising of victimizing children too young to tell the difference between a sales pitch and disinterested advice, and they have assailed what they view as its offensiveness to the elderly, to minorities, and to women. Educators, journalists, and others have often voiced disapproval of advertising: a "torrent of mendacity, imbecility, and bilge" was how author Bernard De Voto characterized it some years ago.

Among advertising's critics are the corporations that pay for it. Witness the following complaint: "I know that half of my advertising budget is wasted. The problem is that I don't know which half." This quip, attributed to John Wanamaker, Frank W. Woolworth, and Lord Leverhulme among others, has gained a permanent place in advertising lore and illustrates the degree to which advertisers themselves, despite the vast sums spent on research, remain skeptical about how effective their advertising dollars really are.

It is, however, worth noting that disingenuous as it often has been, advertising is first of all about persuasion. It has, therefore, been historically far less important in command economies than it has been in market economies. For all its many faults, relative freedom to advertise is an emblem of a more general economic and social freedom. Perhaps it is part of the price we pay for that freedom.

Nature of Advertising

- A public notice meant (a) to convey information and (b) invite patronage or some other response. Inform and persuade ("stimulate demand"). From a marketing context, advertising could be defined as "a paid form of non-personal communication about an organization and / or its products that is transmitted to a target audience through a mass medium." Therefore one kind of promotional activity, separate from publicity (free), sales promotion (not forms of communication), and personal selling (not impersonal nor through a mass medium).
- Morally neutral: Neither in itself good or bad. Reason: Advertising is a tool.

Main Objections to Advertising

- Advertising is deceptive—in whole or in part.
- Advertising weakens or undermines personal autonomy; that some kinds of advertising are immoral. Advertising plays on human desires for security, acceptance, self-esteem to influence consumer choices. John Kenneth Galbraith's: The Dependence Effect—industrial production turns out goods to satisfy wants, and at the same time creates the wants. For example, mouthwash, anti-persperant. So production is no longer justifiable, the market is no longer self-correcting, and human autonomy is undermined.
    - F.A. von Hayek: Almost all wants beyond primitive needs for food, shelter, and sex are the result of cultural influences. Desires for art, music, and literature are created by painters, musicians and novelists. Non-sequitur to hold that wants created by the forces that also satisfy them are less urgent or less important. Worth of a want cannot depend on its source, but on some other criterion.
    - Advertising should not cynically exploit deep-seated emotions or short-circuit logical thought processes. Good advertising appeals on many grounds, aesthetic, intellectual, humorous, heartwarming. But it shouldn't deprive of freedom of choice.
    - Advertising promotes consumption as way of life (Christopher Lasch); it empties communication of its content, destroys credence in

the written or spoken word (Robert Heilbroner); it is (often) tasteless and irritating, and lowers culture in general.

- [Economic objection] Advertising is a waste of resources (adds nothing to the value of consumer products and diverts resources from the production of more valuable goods) and inefficient (enables large firms with well-established brand-name products to create and maintain monopoly conditions), largely a non-productive activity that stifles competition. Which would mean that it actually harms the system in general.
- Advertising increases value of a product by creating buyers of the product, creates an expanding market, and actually has been shown to lower prices. And there is no guarantee that dollars saved on advertising could be utilized more efficiently, especially in a surplus economy.

Ethical Principles

General

- Principles of the moral order must be applied to the domain of media.
- Human freedom has a purpose: making an authentic moral response. All attempts to inform and persuade must respect the purposes of human freedom if they are to be moral.
- Morally good advertising therefore is that advertising that seeks to move people to choose and act rationally in morally good ways; morally evil advertising seeks

to move people to do evil deeds that are self-destructive and destructive of authentic community.

- Means and techniques of advertising must also be considered: manipulative, exploitative, corrupt and corrupting methods of persuasion and motivation.

Three Specific Moral Principles

Respect Truthfulness (Deception Objection)

- Never directly intend to deceive.
- Never use simply untrue advertising.
- Do not distort the truth by implying things that are not so or withholding relevant facts.
- "Puffery" is acceptable where it is consonant with recognized and accepted rhetorical and symbolic practice.

Respect the Dignity of Each Human Person (Attacks Autonomy Objection)

- Do not exploit our "lower inclinations" to compromise our capacity to reflect or decide either through its content or through its impact: using appeals to lust, vanity, envy and greed, and other human weakness.
- Give special care to the weak and vulnerable: children, young people, the elderly, the poor, and the culturally disadvantaged

Respect Social Responsibilities (Promotes Consumption, Empties Communication, Objections)

- Example: Concern for the ecology—advertising should not favour a lavish lifestyle which wastes resources and despoils the environment.

- *Example:* Advertising should not reduce human progress to acquiring material goods and cultivating a lavish lifestyle.

Benefits of Advertising

- *Economic:* Useful tool for sustaining honest and ethically responsible competition by informing people of the availability of rationally desirable new products and services and improvements in existing ones.
- *Political:* Helps counteract tendencies toward the monopolization of power by informing people of the ideas and policy proposals of parties and candidates.
- *Cultural:* Can exert a positive influence on decisions about media content; contribute the betterment of society by uplifting and inspiring people and motivating them to act in ways that benefit themselves and others. Importance of witty, tasteful and entertaining advertising, even to the point of becoming art.
- *Moral and Religious:* Communicate messages of faith, patriotism, tolerance, compassion and neighbourly service, charity, health, education.

Harms of Advertising

- *Economic:* Misrepresent and without relevant facts; subvert the media by pressure not to treat of questions that are embarrassing and inconvenient; tout harmful or useless goods; move people based on non-rational decisions; become a tool of "consumerism"; particularly harmful in economically less developed countries.

- *Political:* Costs of advertising can limit political competition to wealthy candidates or to those willing to compromise their integrity; distorts the views and records of opponents.
- *Cultural:* Corrupt culture and cultural values by contradicting sound traditional values: can create superficiality, tawdriness, and moral squalor; ignore educational and social needs of certain segments of the audience; contributes to stereotyping of particular groups. Moral and religious harms: deliberate appeals to motives of envy, status seeking, and lust creates vulgar and morally degrading advertising; treat of religion in obnoxious and offensive manners; can promote morally suspect or perverse products and practices.

ICC Guidelines on Advertising and Marketing on the Internet April 1998

Principles for Responsible Advertising and Marketing over the Internet, World Wide Web, Online Service Electronic Networks.

Introduction

The global promise of new communications technologies has become a subject of great public interest businesses and governments discuss the best ways of introducing these technologies and of sharing with consumers the benefits they offer. By marrying the user-friendliness of the computer/television screen for instantaneous transmission of telecommunications, these technologies are providing a new means for delivery of information, entertainment and business services, bringing consumers and business closer. Consumers are being empowered, more than ever before, to dialogue with producers and to precisely their particular needs and desires.

Advertisers and marketers are helping to develop the new media just as they helped to develop the traditional media of the past. Today, advertising represents the main source of revenue for traditional media. Similarly advertising and marketing will make a vital contribution to the new interactive media by allowing it to offer affordable goods and services to a wider, global audience.

The International Chamber of Commerce (ICC) is the world's foremost developer of self-regulatory code of ethical conduct for advertising and marketing practices. The ICC believes that advertising and marketing Internet, World Wide Web, and online services should reflect the highest standards of ethical conduct and down in the ICC International Code of Advertising Practice and other relevant ICC self-regulatory Code.

The global character and technological properties of the new media have created a unique business environment. Media owner in the traditional sense, do not exist, which has led to the bypassing of traditional intermediaries such as publishers and broadcasters. Responsible advertisers and marketers (which, in context, will mean any person or company posting an electronic commercial message) should recognize in their own interest to observe self-disciplinary guidelines specifically adapted for electronic or interact advertising and marketing. Advertisers and marketers should strive to create an electronic environment the world's consumers can fully trust.

Consumers and marketers should seek to cooperate in order to minimize the potential cost and to enhance efficiency savings of electronic networks. By choosing to share pertinent data about themselves, consumption be provided with relevant product information and efficient and economical services. This will enable to choose goods and services better adapted to their needs and tastes.

The ICC recognizes that advertising and marketing in the interactive media is at an early stage of development and acknowledges that the relevant principles and guidelines may have to change and evolve as we learn about the new technologies and their specific uses. Thus, in light of experience acquired, the ICC present hereafter an updated version of the 1996 Guidelines. The ICC commits itself to the regular review of the guidelines to ensure their continued viability.

With the above in mind, the ICC recommends the worldwide promulgation of the guidelines below, which to fulfill the following objectives:

- to enhance the confidence of the public at large in advertising and marketing provided over the interactive systems;
- to safeguard an optimum of freedom of expression for advertisers and marketers;
- to minimize the need for governmental and/or inter-governmental legislation or regulations; and
- to meet reasonable consumer privacy expectations.

Scope of the Guidelines

These guidelines apply to all marketing and advertising activities on the Internet for the promotion of a goods or services. The Guidelines set standards of ethical conduct to be observed by all involved with advertising and marketing activities on the Internet.

Definitions

For the purpose of these guidelines:

- the term "Internet" refers to the public network of computer networks which enables the transmission of information between users, or between users and a place on the network, as well as to all internate media and electronic networks such as the World Wide Web and online services;
- the term "content" means all forms of advertising and marketing information and covers text, animation, video and audio, and may also include software;
- the term "World Wide Web" refers to the network of resources accessible on the Internet using Hypertext Transfer Protocol ("http").

Basic Principles

Article 1

All advertising and marketing on the Internet should comply with the spirit as well as the letter of the principle set forth in the ICC's Codes on Advertising Practice, Sales Promotion, Direct Marketing, Environmental Advertising, and Sponsorship as well as the ICC-ESOMAR Code on Marketing and Social Research.

All advertising and marketing should be legal, decent, honest and truthful "Legal", in the context of the guidelines, is presumed to mean that advertising and marketing messages should be legal in their course origin. Advertising and marketing messages should be sensitive to issues of social responsibility and should it conform to generally accepted principles as regards ethical marketing.

Advertising and marketing messages should not be designed or transmitted in such a way as to impair public confidence in the internet as a medium and marketplace.

Rules

Disclosure of Identity

Article 2

Advertisers and marketers of goods and services who post-commercial messages via the Internet should disclose their own identity and that of the relevant subsidiary, if applicable, in such a way that the user contact the advertiser or marketer without difficulty.

Costs and Responsibilities Associated with Electronic Sales and Marketing

Article 3

Advertisers and marketers should clearly inform users of the cost of accessing a message or a service the cost is higher than the basic telecommunications rate. Users should be provided with such notice of the time they are about to access the message or service. This notice mechanism should allow users a reasonable amount of time, as set by the marketer or mandated by applicable law, to disconnect from the service without incurring the charge.

Respect for Public Groups
Article 4

Advertisers and marketers should respect the role of particular electronic news groups, forums or bulletin as public meeting places which may have rules and standards as to acceptable commercial behaviour. Advertising and marketing messages posted to public sites are appropriate.

- when the forum or site receiving the message has a fundamentally commercial nature or activity:
- when the subject or theme of the bulletin board or news group is pertinent to the content of the advertising of marketing message; or
- when the forum or site has otherwise implicitly or explicitly indicated consent to the receipt of a marketing messages.

Users' Rights

Article 5

1. Collection and use of data. Advertisers and marketers should disclose the purpose(s) for collecting and using personal data to users and should not use the data in a way incompatible with those purposes. Data file should be accurate, complete and kept up to date.

2. Data privacy. Advertisers and marketers should take reasonable precautions to safeguard the security of their data files.

3. Disclosure of data. The user should be given the opportunity to refuse the transfer of data to another advertiser or market. Personal data should not be disclosed when the user has objected except by authority of law. Online mechanisms should be put in place to allow users to exercise their right to opt-out by electronic means.

4. Correction and blocking of data. Advertisers and marketers should give the user the right to obtain data relating to him and, where appropriate, to have such data corrected, completed, or blocked.

5. Privacy policy statements. Advertisers and marketers are encouraged to post their privacy policy statement on their online site. When such privacy policy statements exist, they should be easy to find, easy to use and comprehensible.

6. Unsolicited commercial messages. Advertisers and marketers should not send unsolicited commercial messages online to users who have indicated that they do not wish to receive such messages. Advertisers and marketer should make an online mechanism available to users by which the users can make known to the advertisers and marketers that they do not wish to receive future online solicitations. Unsolicited online advertising or marketing commercial messages should be clearly identified as such and should identify the advertiser or marketer.

Advertising to Children

Article 6

Advertisers and marketers offering goods or services to children online should:

- not exploit the natural credulity of children or the lack of experience of young people and should strain their sense of loyalty.
- not contain any content which might result in harm to children.
- identify material intended only for adults.
- encourage parents and/or guardians to participate in and/or supervise their children's online.
- encourage young children to obtain their parent's and/or guardians permission before the child provide information online, and make reasonable efforts to ensure that parental consent is given.
- provide information to parents and/or guardians about ways to protect their children's privacy.

Respect for the Potential Sensitivities of a Global Audience

Article 7

Given the global reach of electronic networks, and the variety and diversity of possible recipients of elementary messages, advertisers and marketers should be especially sensitive regarding the possibility that a message might be perceived as pornographic, violent, racist or sexist.

Note: ICC Codes and Guidelines are always subordinate to existing national law. There is currently no internal unanimity as to whether country of origin or country of destination applies to advertising and marketing internet.

2

Scanning Advertisements

Introduction

The world of advertising seems too good to be true. It has glamour. It offers the best things in life and has quick-fix solutions to almost all problems that consumers may face. Advertising has become such an inextricable pail of our lives–that we can't really imagine life without it.

Advertising is a means by which messages are brought to the attention of the public, through various media, in a persuasive and memorable fashion. It usually focuses on the good parts of the product or service in an effort to get people to buy it. The basic objectives of advertisements are:

- to inform the consumer about new products, product users, services available, or other facts that need to be known by consumers.
- to persuade an audience to purchase a product, change brand preferences, or perceive a product differently.
- to remind consumers about the need for a product or where it may be purchased.

There are more than 70 television channels in India, reaching 24 million cable and satellite homes and with over 150 million viewers. Advertising budgets climb up every year. McDonald's spends 2 billion dollars on advertising alone annually. Consumer goods companies spend anything between 5 to 15 per cent of their turnover on brand building and advertising. The largest consumer goods company in India, HLL spent Rs. 724 crore on advertising in 1999 and Colgate spends almost 18 per cent of its 11 billion turnover on advertising. A large part of the ad spend of the cigarette and liquor majors in the country goes into surrogate advertisements.

Promotional offers are also offered to lure consumers into over-consumption. Almost every product that is being advertised on Indian television comes packaged with a promotional offer–be it a discount, a freebie, a chance to loot a jewellery store for one minute, lakhs of rupees and goodies as prizes, or the possibility of dining and holidaying with celebrities–the whole world is up for grabs on TV.

Negative advertising is another strategy that is being used very extensively by advertisers today. The on-going Cola wars between Pepsi and Coke being a classic example.

Is there a way to determine how much advertising affects our lives and influences our purchase decisions, and goes even further to change our attitudes? Besides, who monitors the subliminal and surrogate advertising that we hardly ever notice and yet, which leaves an indelible mark on our minds? And the most important why advertisements are made in bad taste? Is that essential? Can't the ideas be otherwise effectively communicated?

Some ads made in bad taste and were subsequently taken off air because of pressure from ministers, within the information and broadcasting ministry, from individual bodies or the end viewers themselves who were uncomfortable watching those ads with their family, can be recalled are, an advertisement of a Colgate product in which a prisoner kisses a lady police officer, Kamasutra condom ads where instead of making people aware of the necessity of safe sex and the benefits of birth control, condom ads continue to intrigue the youngsters with the unique feel it has to offer, a tabloid published a photograph of an ad for Tuff shoes that had models Madhu Sapre and Milind Soman posing in the nude with a python wrapped around them, just about covering the vitals. The ad agencies defended their creative rights while the nation pooh-poohed the couple's audacity, Fair and Lovely cream ad that imply that a woman, whether in kitchen or in the boardroom, ought to look sensuous and inviting under any circumstances. The fairness creams stereotype the dusky women as socially less desired for marriage and job. Are advertisers free to use any form of advertising to push their sales?

Doctors say intake of anything other than mother's milk in the first six months leads to pseudo-faltering or uneven growth and a variety of afflictions like diarrhea, chest infection and sore throat. But most commercials promote its use in the fourth month, which is both misleading and violate the Infant Milk Substitute, Feeding Bottles and Infant Foods Act. Irrespective of their education standard, women in both rural and urban areas are influenced by the "healthy baby-happy mother" commercials of the corporate persuading them to opt for infant milk and allied products.

Unethical ads are often found to have negative consequences, ranging from adverse publicity to diminished corporate reputation, to consumer boycotts and even legal sanctions. Conversely, an ethical ad can contribute to a good corporate reputation, heighten morale and, thus, increase repeat business.

In India, rules pertaining to advertising are very lax. Also, there are no regulatory bodies that monitor TV advertisements. Apart from the Ministry of Information and Broadcasting that decides to intervene when it wants to, there are only voluntary groups like the Advertising Agencies Association of India, and the Advertising Standards Council of India, both of which are business organisations and can only put moral pressure on advertisers and companies to withdraw objectionable advertisements.

India may have made great progress in the area of free trade, entry of multinationals in the country and in Information Technology but monitoring of the content of advertisements and marketing of products on television still remains very poor. Advertisers blatantly target young consumers for consumption of their nutritionally harmful products like fast food.

People in government believe in self-regulation and are not in favour of enforcement by the Government. Government says professional organizations like ASCI must exercise their influence in motivating their member advertisers to conform to their own code for observing decency, legality, honesty, truthfulness and respectability. All of us who professionally use the mass media are the shapers of the society. We can vulgarize that society. We can brutalize it. Or we can help lift it onto a higher level.

A Study

Aim

To analyse advertisements which are bad in taste, unethical and portraying women as a sex symbol.

Objectives

- To find the awareness level of people about controversial advertisement.
- To find wether people approve these advertisements.
- To find do people want some regulations regarding ads or want some ads to be banned.
- To find the effect of these banned advertisements on viewership.

Findings

- 73 per cent of people in our study are aware of controversial advertisements whereas 27 per cent are ignorant about the controversies surrounding various ads.
- 61 per cent of people in our sample approve that these advertisements are controversial whereas a 15 per cent says that these controversies are baseless and 24 per cent could not form an opinion.
- A large part of sample 15 per cent said that these ads do not have any affect on the viewers. 55 per

cent says that it leaves a negative affects whereas to 30 per cent had an opinion that such advertisements have positive affect on viewers.

- 94 per cent people said banning of such ads is justified, a majority of which, 34 per cent, said such ads should be banned because of their presentation then 42 per cent said because of their content and 24 per cent said idea was their reason, there were 6 per cent people who said controversial ads or ads in bad taste should not be banned.
- 40 per cent of people want regulation of advertisements to some extent, 38 per cent said, yes, there should be some regulation and 11 per cent do not want any sort of regulations on advertisements.

Conclusion

A large number of people were found to be aware of controversial advertisement such as an advertisement of a Colgate product in which a prisoner kisses a lady police officer, Kamasutra condom ads where the ad continue to intrigue the youngsters with the unique feel it has to offer, an ad for Tuff shoes that had models posing in the nude with a python wrapped around them, just about covering the vitals. Fair and Lovely cream ad that imply that a woman, whether in kitchen or in the boardroom, ought to look sensuous and inviting under any circumstances. Unethical ads are often found to have negative consequences.

It was also found that a large section of society wants some sort of regulation be it self-regulation or by the government authorities.

People are also in favour of showing ads related to kids products during kids programmes. And they also believed that banning of above-mentioned ads is justified, moreover ads in bad taste or showing any sort of negative presentation for personal profits, such as boosting of sales, in relation to our environment, or ads which target a section of society or divide society on any basis such as Fair and Lovely ad did on the basis of colour, should be banned. This is for the simple reason that 41 per cent people think that such ads have negative affect, but on other hand 48 per cent took a neutral stand on this.

DIAMONDS
ARE AS
PRECIOUS
AS YOUR LOVE
Complementing the beauty and
grace of woman in you
Only for one close to your heart...
A Diamond Can Talk
Hundred of Words
Only the purest diamond
can glow your beauty
DIAMOND HUT
Symbol of Love
Exclusive Designer's Diamond Jewellery
2883/17, Regent Tower, Hardian Singh Road
Karol Bagh, New Delhi-110005
Phone: 25729416, 51545630, 51545635,
9811050100; Fax: 25729436;
E-mail: info@diamondhutindia.com
Website: www.diamondhutindia.com

3

Advertising Media, Agency Impact

Advertising

Advertising is a message designed to promote a product, a service, or an idea. In many countries, people come into daily contact with many kinds of advertising. Printed advertisements make up a large part of newspapers and magazines. Poster advertisements appear in many buses, and in shops and other public buildings. Commercials are advertisements, which interrupt TV and radio programmes. Other types of advertisements are called adverts or ads.

The purpose of most advertising is to sell products or services. Manufacturers advertise to try to persuade people to buy their products. Large business firms also use advertising to create a favourable "image" of their company. They want the company name to be known and respected for the products the firm makes or the services it provides. Local businesses use advertising to gain new customers and increase sales. Advertising thus plays a part in the competition among businesses. It is the cheapest and fastest way to inform large numbers of people about products or services for sale and to persuade them to buy. In many businesses, the volume of sales depends largely on the amount of advertising done.

Individuals, political parties and candidates, social organizations, special-interest groups, and governments also use advertising. Many people advertise in newspapers to sell used cars, homes, or other property. Political parties and candidates use advertising to try to win votes. Special-interest groups and government bodies often advertise to promote a cause or to influence the way people think or act. Some of their advertisements provide a public service. For example, in some countries public service ads are designed to discourage people from smoking.

The United States has the world's largest advertising industry. Television commercials take up more viewing time than in other countries. Advertising pays all television and radio costs. Other countries with large advertising industries include France, Germany, Japan, and the United Kingdom.

Where advertising is widespread it has enormous influence on people's lives. Advertising encourages people to eat certain foods, wear certain clothes, drive certain cars, and use certain household products. It promotes the use of labour-saving appliances and then suggests ways to enjoy the resulting leisure time. In doing all these things, advertising helps shape tastes, habits, attitudes, and culture of a country. In promoting the sale of many kinds of goods, advertising can help raise the standard of living.

Advertising is common in almost all countries. In many countries, however, the use of advertising is restricted. In most countries of Western Europe, for example, the governments limit the amount of advertising on television and the types of product, which may be advertised. In Norway and Sweden television advertising is illegal.

Advertising Media

Advertising reaches people through various forms of mass communication. These media include newspapers, magazines, television, and radio. Advertisers buy space in newspapers and magazines to publish their ads. They buy time on television and radio to broadcast their commercials. National advertisers, such as airlines and food companies, use the media to reach consumers throughout large parts of the country or all of it. Local advertisers, such as departmental stores, supermarkets, and restaurants, use the media to reach consumers within a district or town.

The chief advertising media are (1) Newspapers, (2) Magazines, (3) Direct mail, (4) Radio, (5) Television, and (6) Outdoor signs. Newspapers and TV receive the largest share of the money spent on advertising.

Newspapers

Newspapers offer advertisers several advantages over other media. Most adults read a daily newspaper, and many of them specifically check the ads for information about products, services, or special sales. Daily newspapers also offer the advantage of timeliness. An advertiser can prepare and publish an advertisement within a day. Newspaper ads can thus quickly reflect a sudden demand for certain merchandise or use a theme that relates to current news.

Newspapers carry two main kinds of advertisements: display ads and classified ads. Display ads range in size from less than 2.5 centimetres to a full page or more, and most include illustrations. Advertisers can appeal to people with special interests by placing their ads on certain pages, such as those devoted to travel, home life, or sports. Classified ads appear in a separate section of a newspaper. Most classified ads consist of a few lines of print. The ads list homes, used cars, furniture, and other property that individuals have for sale. Used-car dealers, and firms with job vacancies also place classified ads. Some newspapers will also accept preprinted ad sections called free-standing inserts, which are several pages long.

Magazines

Magazines have a number of advantages over newspapers as an advertising medium. They are usually read in a leisurely manner and are often kept for weeks or months before being discarded. In many cases, several members of a family read each copy of a magazine. Another advantage of magazines is that they offer better printing and colour reproduction than newspapers do. Advertisers can thus show off their products to greater advantage in magazines.

Advertisers can choose from a wide variety of magazines. Some magazines, such as news magazines, appeal to a mass audience. Others are designed for specific groups of people, such as teenagers, home-makers, or amateur photographers. Certain companies advertise in trade publications, which are devoted to particular businesses, industries, or professions. For example, advertisers who sell agricultural equipment and supplies use farm magazines.

Direct Mail

Direct mail includes leaflets, brochures, catalogues, and other printed advertisements that are delivered by a postal service. Mail-order firms, which sell largely through the mail, are the main users of direct mail advertising. Companies that have mail-order departments, and many companies that do not, also advertise by direct mail.

The effectiveness of advertising by direct mail depends mainly on the quality of the mailing list. Some lists consist of all the addresses in a city or a large area and are simply sent to "Occupant." Other mailing lists consist of individual names with addresses. Some firms specialize in preparing lists of people according to their occupation, age, income, interests, or other characteristics. For example, a firm might assemble a list of 20,000 new mothers or 10000 lawyers. These lists are sold to advertisers. Some advertisers assemble their own lists.

Direct mail advertising costs more per person reached than do other ways of advertising. However, advertisers who obtain special mailing lists know they are reaching good prospects. In addition, advertisers can choose from many different sizes and forms of advertisements. Some products or services are too complicated to be explained in any other medium.

Radio

One advantage of advertising on radio is that people can listen to programmes while doing other things, such as driving a car or working at home. Another advantage is that radio audiences, in general, are more highly selected by the type of programming than are television audiences. For example, stations that feature country music attract different kinds of listeners than do those that play rock or pop music. By selecting the station, advertisers can reach the people most likely to buy their products. Radio commercials include direct sales announcements, dramatized stories, and songs. The majority of commercials last 30 to 60 seconds.

Television

A main advantage of television to advertisers is that it brings sight, sound, and action directly to consumers in their homes. Advertisers can explain their products to viewers who are enjoying a TV programme and cannot easily avoid the commercials. In addition, television reaches a vast, nationwide audience. Although advertising time on television is expensive, the cost per person reached is low.

Television commercials can be broadcast from film, or from videotape. Filmed or videotaped commercials are recorded in a studio or at another location. The commercials may use performers in true-to-life situations, such as a family around the dinner table or a group of people at a party. Some TV commercials consist of animation.

The majority of TV commercials last 30 seconds. The commercials are usually run in groups of three to six. In most countries, the government limits television commercial time to a set number of minutes per hour. For example, in Britain commercials are limited to about 6 minutes per hour during prime time and 9 minutes per hour during most other broadcast times. Prime time refers to the evening hours, when TV programmes draw the largest audience.

Outdoor Signs

One of the main advantages of outdoor signs is that people pass by the signs repeatedly. In addition, large, colourful signs easily attract attention. However, the ads on outdoor signs must be short and simple because most passers-by see a sign for only a few seconds.

The main kinds of outdoor signs are (1) posters, (2) painted bulletins, and (3) electric spectaculars. Posters, commonly called billboards, are the most widely used form of outdoor advertising. They consist of printed sheets of paper, which are pasted on large billboards. Painted bulletins are signs painted on buildings or billboards. Electric spectaculars consist of large illuminated displays. Many feature changing messages and moving pictures. Electric spectaculars are the most expensive kind of outdoor sign.

Other ways of advertising include the use of (1) transportation signs, (2) window displays, (3) point-of-sale displays, (4) telephone directories, and (5) novelties.

Transportation signs are small posters placed in or on local trains, buses, and taxicabs. Posters placed inside vehicles can carry a longer message than outside ads because riders have more time to read it.

Window displays are designed to attract customers into a shop. Many shops have a promotion department, whose duties include preparing window displays. Other shops hire display firms. Many manufacturers give display materials to shops that sell their products.

Point-of-sale displays are arrangements of signs, banners, and other items within a shop. The displays draw attention to certain products and are designed to encourage impulse buying that is, buying on the spur of the moment. The materials for most point-of-sale displays are supplied by the manufacturers of the products being advertised.

Telephone directories in some countries carry ads in a section called the yellow pages. Some of the ads consist of a few printed lines that give the name, address, and telephone number of local businesses. Others take up more space and are like display ads in newspapers and magazines.

Novelties are inexpensive items that many advertisers give away. Such items include calendars, matchbooks, and key rings that carry an advertiser's name and message. People are reminded of the advertiser as long as they use the item.

Advertising Techniques

Advertising is designed to inform, influence, or persuade people. To be effective, an advertisement must first attract attention and gain a person's interest. It may then provide reasons for buying a product and for believing the advertiser's claims.

Advertisers use a variety of techniques to create effective advertisements. They start with a basic appeal, which is the main selling point, or theme, of an advertisement. They then use certain specific techniques. The most commonly used techniques include (1) attention-getting headlines, (2) slogans, (3) testimonials,

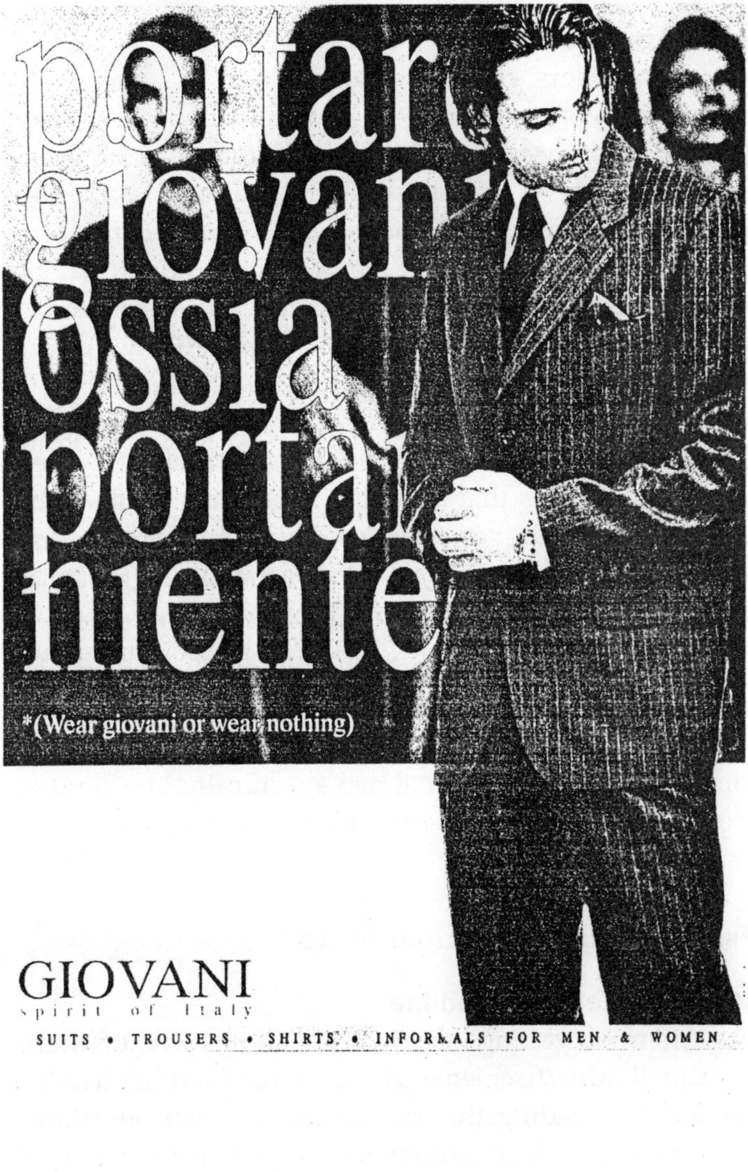
portar
giovan
ossia
portar
niente
*(Wear giovani or wear nothing)
GIOVANI
spirit of Italy
SUITS • TROUSERS • SHIRTS • INFORMALS FOR MEN & WOMEN

(4) product characters, (5) comparison of products, and (6) repetition.

Basic Appeals

Advertisers rely on many kinds of appeals to persuade people to buy. In general, advertisers may present their message either in a factual way or in an emotional way. Advertisements that use a factual approach describe the demonstrable characteristics of a product. Such ads tell what the product is, how it works, or how it is made. Advertisements that use an emotional appeal stress the ways in which a product will give personal satisfaction. Such an ad might appeal to a person's need for love, security, or prestige and suggest that the product will satisfy the need. Advertisers often use sexual themes that appeal to a person's desire to be attractive to the opposite sex. For example, an advertisement for after shave lotion might suggest that the product will help a man attract women.

To persuade the largest possible number of people, many advertisements combine factual information with an emotional appeal, or they use several appeals. In some cases, the appeal is aimed specifically at a limited group of people, such as business executives or young married couples.

Print Media Advertisements

Attention Getting Headline

Attention getting headlines are an important feature of printed advertisements. A successful headline leads a person into reading the rest of the ad. Some headlines attract attention by promising the reader a personal benefit, such as a saving in money or an improvement in physical appearance. Other headlines are cleverly worded to arouse a person's curiosity. Still other headlines carry news, such as an announcement of a new product. Headlines also attract attention by directly addressing a specific group. For example, a headline might read: "For the Young Single Woman." The opening lines in a radio or TV commercial serve the same purpose as headlines in printed ads.

Slogans are short phrases that a company uses over and over in its ads. Good slogans are easy to remember and tend to stick in people's minds. The majority of slogans are designed to help create a favourable image of a company and its products. Most such slogans do not relate to particular features of a product. Companies also use slogans in advertising inexpensive products, such as chewing gum or soft drinks.

Testimonials are advertisements in which a person endorses a product. The person may be someone who looks like an average user of the product. Advertisers also pay film and TV stars, popular athletes, and other celebrities to endorse products. A celebrity helps attract attention to an advertisement. In addition, endorsement by a celebrity can be persuasive if the person's public image suits the product. People may then trust the celebrity's word and be influenced to buy the product. In some countries, government regulations compel endorsers to use the advertised product if they claim they do so.

Product characters are fictional people and animals or characters that are used in advertisements over a long period. Many advertisers use product characters to deliver sales messages for a whole line of products. The characters become highly familiar to people and so provide lasting identification with a company's products. Product characters are often used in advertising aimed at children because such characters delight many youngsters.

Comparison of products is used most frequently to sell products that compete heavily with other brands. Advertisers compare their product with similar brands and point out the advantages of using their brand. A competitor's product may be named or hinted at, or it may be referred to as "Brand X" or "another leading brand."

Repetition is one of the most basic techniques advertisers use to get their message across. Advertisers may broadcast their commercials several times a day for weeks on TV or radio. Or they may publish their ads frequently in printed media. Repetition can help build or reinforce a company's reputation. Advertisers also believe that the more often people see or hear an advertisement, the more likely they are to accept the message and want the product.

Role of Advertising Agency

Creating Advertisements

Most business firms hire advertising agencies to create their advertisements and place them in the various media. In most cases, individual advertisements form part of an advertising campaign. A campaign is an organized sales effort that may run for several months and that usually involves more than one medium.

In planning an advertising campaign, the agency must first determine the objective of the campaign. The objective may be to prove a product's superiority over competing brands, to change the image of the company, or to achieve some other goal. The agency must also determine the target market—that is, the people who are likely users of a product and at whom the advertising will be aimed. Finally, the agency has to estimate how much money and time will be needed to carry out the campaign.

Large advertising agencies generally assign a team of persons from the various departments of the agency to handle all the advertising for a specific advertiser, or client. The typical agency includes a account department research department, creative department, media department, and production department. An account manager, or account executive, has overall responsibility for planning and directing a client's advertising. The following discussion describes in broad terms the way an agency creates advertisements. The main steps include (1) research, (2) media selection, (3) creative work, and (4) production.

Research

Information gathered from consumers provides the basis for many advertising decisions. It helps an agency determine the kinds of people at whom to aim advertisements, the types of appeals to use, and in which media to place the ads. Various kinds of research are conducted by the agency's research department, by the client, or by marketing research firms.

Market research seeks information about consumers and their buying habits. The information is obtained from consumers by means of surveys, questionnaires, and interviews. Such information helps advertisers decide on the best way to present their products.

Motivation research tries to find out why people buy certain products. Motivation researchers gather information in interviews, during which they use techniques developed by psychologists and sociologists.

Media Selection

The members of an agency's media department compare the various media in terms of audience size and make up. They decide which particular medium to use to reach the target market.

Creative Work

Creative work is probably the most important part of an advertising campaign. An agency's creative department develops the theme of an advertising campaign and designs individual advertisements.

For printed advertisements, a copywriter prepares the copy (written words) and an artist prepares a layout of the advertisement. A layout is a sketch that shows the placement of the copy and illustrations.

For radio commercials, a copywriter prepares the script, which may consist of a sales message or dialogue and perhaps sound effects or background music.

For television commercials, a copywriter creates the script and an artist designs a storyboard, which is a series of drawings of the planned action. The storyboard is combined with the script and includes directions for filming the commercial.

Production

The production of printed advertisements, radio commercials, and TV commercials is arranged by the production department of an advertising agency. For printed advertisements, the production department works inhouse or with graphic arts firms, which set the copy in type and prepare the necessary printing plates of the type and illustrations. For radio commercials, the production department selects performers to read the commercial and the commercial is then recorded on tape in a studio.

For television commercials, the agency hires a film or video producer. After the commercial is shot, it must be combined with the sound track and edited. The production department delivers the finished commercial to the TV stations or network where it will be aired.

Effects of Advertising

Advertising can influence many aspects of life. This section deals with some of its economic, social, and political effects.

Economic Effects

Advertising plays a major role in the distribution of goods from manufacturers to consumers. It provides an effective way for sellers to inform buyers about products. Advertising thus helps manufacturers sell their products.

Advertising also helps the economy grow by stimulating demand for new products. Manufacturers spend much money to develop new products. Through advertising, they can speed up the process of creating a market for a product and so recover their costs more quickly. Fewer new products would be developed if manufacturers could not use advertising to help sell the products.

Some economists believe that a large amount of the money spent on advertising is wasted. They argue that much advertising simply leads consumers to switch from one brand of a product to another brand. Brand switching may increase the profits of a particular firm but has no positive effect on the overall economy.

Advertisers include the expense of advertising in the sales price of a product. In some cases, advertising raises the price of a product. In other cases, advertising helps lower prices by creating the mass demand that supports mass production, which is cheaper.

Social Effects

Perhaps the most important social contribution of advertising is that it supports the mass communication media. Advertising pays all the costs of commercial television and radio. It provides viewers with free entertainment and news programmes. Advertising also pays two-thirds of the costs of newspapers and magazines. Without advertising, readers would have to pay a higher price for them, and many of the publications would go out of business.

Because the mass media depend on advertising, many people question whether advertisers control the media. Newspapers and magazines have separate editorial and advertising departments. Generally, they do not allow advertisers to influence the editorial content of the publications. However, many publications do not hesitate to print favourable information about their advertisers, and they sometimes refuse to print unfavourable information. Critics of commercial television maintain that dependence on advertising lowers the quality of TV programming.

In order to sell advertising time at high prices, TV stations try to attract the largest possible audience. Critics argue that the stations therefore broadcast too many general entertainment programmes and not enough informational and cultural programmes.

Many critics also charge that advertising persuades people to buy products they do not need or want through the use of psychological techniques. Advertisers reply that they do not have the means to make people buy unwanted products. They argue that adults freely choose what to buy or what not to buy. Most experts agree, however, that advertising is particularly persuasive to young children, who do not have the ability or experience to judge advertising critically.

Political Effect

Little attention was paid to political advertising, apart from billboards, until 1952, when Dwight D. Eisenhower successfully ran for the US presidency. Advertising executives, rather than politicians, directed Eisenhower's presidential campaign. Much of the campaign consisted of a flood of announcements on television stations.

Since 1952, advertising executives have played an increasingly important role in political campaigns in many countries. In addition advertising has become a major feature of campaigns for public offices at the national and state levels. The chief criticism of political advertising concerns the use of such announcements. In many cases, these brief messages concentrate on creating an image of a candidate and tend to oversimplify the issues. Critics object to candidates being "sold" through advertising methods like those used to sell products. Another complaint is that candidates with the most money to spend on advertising have an unfair advantage over their opponents. Because of these objections political advertising on television or radio is illegal in many countries. Also, laws may limit the amount of money that may be spent on any kind of advertising for a political candidate.

4
Sex in Advertising

Indian Mindsets About Sexuality

Indian Sexuality: The Truth and the Surreality

The word sex connotes very strange, strong and acidic reactions among Indian people and they are unable to discuss it and most even deny it. To find out why this unnatural and rather uncomfortable and nerve stirring occurs, we need to probe deeper into the Indian psyche.

It is the conditioning, upbringing and a major historical block for lack of adequate education and formal or informal training in this vital field that is a major reason for sex being such a taboo in India.

Modern Indian Concept of Sex

The modern Indian concept of sex is considered a hidden, occult phenomenon and something to be ashamed of and never to be talked in public. The western Judeo-Christian societies meanwhile have attempted to free themselves by open discussion of such subjects in last few decades thus making it an issue as almost part of the formal education. This has also helped them to clear many doubts, find answers, resolving many material issues and creating an awareness for sexually transmitted diseases.

THE TRENDSETTER
Sairo Mohan, the look that redefined beauty

Having an Asian face is commercially viable for international brands to tap the lucrative Asian markets.

... GLORY
Ujjwala Raut, the face of Yves Saint Laurent cosmetics in '03

to New York, where she now works. Sonalika Sahay has been chosen as the face of Christian Dior watches and will participate in the Beijing Fashion Week this November. Earlier this year, Metropolitan model Monikangana Dutta also got a break with Parisian brands like Christian Dior, Ungaro and Chantall.

There's more good news. Ford Models' Super Model of the World contest is to be revived this year in India. The winner will get a three-year contract for $250,000 (Rs 1.14 crore) apart from immense international exposure.

Indian models had found decent work overseas since the 1970s, but the successes of Anjali Mendes and, later, Shyamoli Varma were exceptions. The international fashion world only really noticed when models like Ujjwala, Sheetal Mallar, Vidisha Pavate and Laxmi Menon would follow, earning substantial international experience at different stages of the 1990s. Ujjwala made it big after she was selected to model at the prestigious Igedo fashion fair at Dusseldorf, Germany. Jesse Randhawa also had the honour of walking the ramp there, apart from working with Nevs and Sodamm Tuff in London for seven months

an attitude
LONGINES
L'ELEGANCE DU TEMPS DEPUIS 1832

Sex and Pornography

India prohibits the publication of pornography but in the zeal to keep pornography in check, the system also bulldozes the really essential and educational information too. This is another thing that many a clever and unprepared people have, in last many years, used educational publications as a cover but they are distributing crude and unsophisticated pornography in the name of discussion and education. Even most of the search engines on the net receive numerous sex-related queries. Unfortunately, most Internet sex-related sites offer nothing but a bunch of pornographic pictures and that even for a price. Most of the people who are unable to get a date, or are frustrated enough to not go out and find one or others who simply believe that they may get some excitement by such voyeurism. For what you can get for a few Rupees worth printed magazines, you pay exorbitant fees to view online. In the other countries, most such people are either teenagers or old people who use these sites for curiosity and anyone with a sense of reality shun this kind of time-waste.

Coming back to India and Indian people's attitude towards sex, the first available thing to almost any Indian person is Film Music and our grotesque movies–which exploit this matter rather sadistically.

Indian film-makers are a rare breed of people who are convinced that people will be greatly excited by seeing a well endowed woman, a man without a shirt, or with breasts padded with wonder bras and cotton, in wet clothes, under artificial rain or on the beach and about a dozen disgusting and absolutely cheap musical gyrations which are denominated as dances.

The lyrics from these movies are used to communicate the imposed censor on sexual expression and to arouse sensual mysteries. Most of the Hindi songs specially written for these movies are nothing but pornography lyricized by seductive vocabulary. This causes more damage than good and this kind of ignorance and hypocrisy is nothing but an unknown tear in the Indian mind. The fears of sex go to hilarious and scary levels. This is actually causing a lot of distress, ignorance and social upheaval in very subtle ways and we need to overcome this stupid notion that discussing sex is unhealthy and unholy.

Changes in the Attitude Towards Sex

The India of last fifty years, has seen great changes and from a virtual zero we started and almost everybody was resourceless and poor. But sheer hard work, we have survived the onslaughts of a Victorian morality. We had to live within our borders and we had to survive and breathe.

Times and things change anyway and global oriented economy has started throwing some lights on the dark corners like India in a way which we never imagined a decade ago. The famous Indian sensuality, quoted incessantly in the world by mentions of Tantric lifestyles, Kamasutras and erotic arts–will change the face of the world, again, in the coming years when Indian people find themselves again.

Use of Sex Appeal in Advertising

Sex: A Biological Process

Sex is the second strongest of the psychological appeals, right behind self-preservation. Its strength is biological and instinctive, the genetic imperative of reproduction. However, its effectiveness and application are gender linked. The differences in male and female psychobiology cause different approaches to and perceptions of sex, both the act and its outcome. Sexual desire is an instinctive reaction in animals, and an individual's perception of a suitable mate is the basis. That perception, usually is a set of criteria that the opposite sex must meet, or at least approximate. An individual regards a member of the opposite gender that meets or exceeds (at least, within the available pool of possibilities) those criteria as being superior to others of that gender. It is therefore the individual that will provide the chance for the highest quality offspring with the best chance of survival. When a possibility doesn't meet the criteria, sexual desire does not occur. Thus, a man's biological criteria can be simple:

1. She must be healthy;
2. She must be young;
3. She must be receptive;
4. And she must be impregnable.

The sex act is of paramount importance to the man; it is how he impregnates the woman.

Sex Appeal in Advertising

What does all this have to do with sex in advertising? The purpose of advertising is to convince people that products are of use to them in one way or another. If people agree, they will buy them. However, advertising must do its job very quickly; it doesn't have the time or the space to go into detail or explanations.

For many products it is possible to find (or invent) a sexual connection. However, the sexual connection is much easier to set up for men than for women. Remember that men have minimal criteria for sexual desire; basically, they are concerned with a woman's anatomy — as long as a woman looks, young enough and healthy, she is desirable. Men also consider her beautiful, since to a male beautiful and sexually attractive are virtually synonymous.

Thus, in advertising it is easy to get a man's attention by using women's bodies and associate getting the woman if he buys the product. It is playing on his instinctive rather than intellectual view of the world. The ad spends no time discussing her qualifications for sexual desire—her mere existence is enough.

Mitigating the instinctive view is the intellectual; most men are aware that women are less concerned with mere anatomy. Women are looking for more. Thus, advertising can show the woman and sell the product on the basis of "women want this [product] in a man. Get the product, get the woman."

The use of sex in advertising to women is a much more difficult proposition. Although they do have an instinctive sexual reaction, their intelligence strongly affects it at the same time. The use of healthy, fit men may indeed attract their attention and create desire, but their willingness to engage in intercourse is rarely aroused strictly because of a man's body. For a woman, sexual desire is a complex mixture of factors, most of which are extremely difficult to inject into an ad in the time and space available. A man's physical appearance plays a role, suggesting health and strength, but her instinctive concern is the long-run, not the short-term. She must see that he is capable not only of sexual activity, but can father healthy children, support and nurture her during pregnancy and birth, and herself and the child after birth, plus assure that the child will be better off than any competition it might have. Many of these factors are also learned in the culture and society. Money, power, prestige, etc., are factors that culture defines as extremely valuable (although rarely placed in the context of being valuable to future children). The woman learns their importance and adds them to her criteria for male sexual desirability. Again, please note that she rarely consciously considers these factors when selecting which man to examine for his suitability as a mate. She will, though, often consciously consider them when deciding whether or not to have sex with him.

However, these factors are almost impossible to put in any one ad; there is not enough time or space to set up the appeal and sell the product.

Finally, lets remember the story of Ms. and Mr. 'Primate' where sex and aggression became linked to a certain degree by Mr. Primate changing his technique. However, for Ms. Primate, he directed the aggression at her – she was the victim. Over the years (and it must have been hundreds of thousands of years), hard-wired into her brain must have been the connection of the sex act and aggression. That she didn't enjoy it didn't matter as long as she got pregnant and had offspring; nature doesn't worry about enjoyment and convenience, just results.

Thus, it is rare for advertising to use sex as an appeal for women. Unlike men (who must enjoy sex to achieve orgasm and thus impregnate the woman), women are often less interested in the sex act itself for its own sake. They are interested in sex for what it can mean in the future. They may enjoy it as much as men, but for them it has a far greater significance. Advertising cannot take advantage of a woman's instinctive sexual desire, because advertising job is not to build for the future—it is to sell a product now.

To sell to a woman, advertising relies on that modern idea (only a few hundred years old) about how men and women relate—romance. Romance fits into the woman's intellectual view of relationships since its major element, courtship, the process by which men apply to be and women select mates, is the discovery of how the male does or does not satisfy her societal criteria for a suitable sexual partner. Rarely does the romantic appeal contain the blatant sexual messages that appear in ads aimed at men since such messages would counter the intellectual view. Although an ad may use a man's body as an attention-getting device, he is usually shown in a romantic rather than sexual context.

Thus, it is clear that sex is a strong appeal to use in advertising. However, it is a gender-linked appeal. Sex easily sells to men; it is an adjunct to women.

How does all this Work in Practice?

Obviously, it depends on the product. Advertisers aim products and services at a specific audience, a target, those most likely to buy the product or service. Since many products or services are intended for one gender or the other, the use of sex appeal varies.

For ads aimed at women, they can achieve the romance approach through using stereotypical images:

roses, soft light and music, a doting man (often a bit bumbling and thus endearing). The ad sells the product on the basis that its purchase will give the woman this feeling of romance in her life.

Example, for perfume: A woman walks along a street. An attractive man smells her perfume and begins chasing after her, often stumbling and bumbling like a puppy. He quickly buys a bouquet of flowers and, when he catches up to her, hands the flowers with a look of adoration. She smiles at him condescendingly and continues walking, pleased with his reaction, as he stands and watches her go. Changes in advertising are, of course, changing as society changes. As you may recall from above, women in today's society are much more liberated in their sexual moves than they have been in millennia past. Advertising, realizing this change in women's perception of sex and sexual activity, is beginning to alter its approach to sex as a selling tool to women.

Note there is little indication of actual sex in these examples. The ad may suggest it as a possibility, but not a certainty simply because of the product. What is certain is that any suggestion of sex is subtle and non-threatening, with the woman in total control, attracting men's attention but not arousing them.

For ads aimed at men, courtship and romance are not a primary approach. Instead, the approach is sex without any complications or difficulties.

Let us take, for example, beer. According to demographics, men rather than women buy and drink the most beer. Therefore, it makes sense for most beer advertising to aim at men. Also, since most beers are parity items (there is little difference between one brand and another), to make a particular brand more appealing to the consumer than another, the ads must induce the difference between them.

With sex appeal the second strongest appeal, it makes sense to use it to make a certain beer more attractive to males (it's difficult to show how drinking beer will keep you alive). The easiest way to do this is to show how attractive a man can be to beautiful women if he drinks that beer.

This is not to imply that all beer commercials use sex to differentiate their products; many usé self-esteem, personal enjoyment, or even altruism. Nonetheless, sex is a powerful and easy method of getting male attention and making their product desirable.

Note that in all the ads, there is no indication that the women are anything but beautiful (i.e., sexually desirable) and become receptive because the men are drinking a particular beer. They don't speak, show no signs of money, position, power or intellect—they are simply beautiful. Although our culture considers deeming mere physical appearance as all that is necessary to make a woman desirable sexist and demeaning to women, the fact remains that for a male it is all that is necessary, an inheritance of biological nature.

A man's eye is attracted to and follows a woman's face and form, not the fact she carries Philip Kotler or a physician's bag, puts money in the Cry fund, or drives an expensive car. None of these make a woman sexually desirable in and of themselves: if they did. Mother Teresa would have replaced. Marilyn Monroe as a sex symbol.

Although the former clearly have intelligence, generosity, compassion and/or money, it is the latter that men lust after.

Occasionally, ads will use innuendo and double entendre in the copy. For example, I recently saw an ad with the headline, "You can't win if you don't stick it in,"(MTV Rock the Vote) clearly carrying a connotation of sexual activity. The ad was promoting voting, and carried an illustration of a hand putting a ballot in a box.

But is it wrong to use sex as a selling tool, especially the way it is used to attract the attention and try to sell to men through their biological attraction to women's bodies? It depends on how you define sexual attraction. If you do it biologically, it is right. If you do it culturally, it is wrong (depending on your culture). Biologically, the purpose of being male is to become aroused by and impregnate as many viable females as possible. For a male, the criterion that a female must meet is to be sexually arousing—nothing else is important.

Culturally, there is a difference. The difference is that the male must satisfy the female's criteria for being sexually attractive. Please note the wording: for a male, sexual arousal is important; for the female, sexual attractiveness is important. There is a difference. For a male, he must be sexually aroused to fulfill his biological function. A human male must have an erection and maintain it through orgasm. If he fails in either, he fails in his biological function.

For the female, on the other hand, arousal is not as important as receptiveness, which she achieves through finding the male sexually attractive. There is no biological need for her either to take pleasure in the sex act or achieve orgasm. If she can arouse the male, she fulfills her biological part of the sex act. Beyond that, her biological function is to get pregnant, give birth, and nurture the offspring.

However, in the human cultural world, which often subordinates biology to intellect, this dichotomy between male and female views of sex can cause friction. Women find men regarding them as "sex objects", considering them sexually attractive strictly on their physical appearance, with no regard for their intelligence or status as equal human beings, offensive and demeaning.

Men find women regarding them as insensitive louts because they respond to billion-year-old instincts over which they have no control, and having women demand they suppress and ignore those instincts, offensive and demeaning. Since neither gender can alter their instincts, they must alter their intellectual views. This is easier for women, since such a major part of their instinctive sexual response is societal and intellectual to start with. Men are making a great effort to overlay their automatic responses with societal and cultural regards.

Thus, the use of sex in, advertising is a two edged sword. Although it is extremely powerful and effective when aimed at one gender, it often does so at the social expense of the other. Since humans live in a social world, consideration must be given to the feelings of the people in that world. If advertising uses the sex appeal, it must be carefully aimed and tastefully done. There is no sense in appealing to one sex by offending the other.

But Sex is Everywhere

In the mid to late 1960s, advertising executives discovered the road to fortune–this road is sex. Especially in present-day society, it is abundantly clear that sex is what sells. We find it on television, in magazines, billboards and even the radio. It seems that everywhere we look, sex is right in front of us.

There is a struggle among advertisers, or at least there should be on whether to use the sure way to sell the maximum number of products or to be true to a sense of morality. More often than not, greed takes over and morality goes out the window. To sell products advertisers target an audience and try to appeal to their senses and feelings. The problem is that sexual appeal seems to be showing up more often with a broader range of products and audiences. Females are more likely than males to be presented in seductive fashions or appear nude but males are now being portrayed as sex symbols more and more.

Despite uncertainty over advertisement effectiveness, the use of sex appeal is still considered an effective method of selling products because of its ability to attract consumer attention to an ad. Advertising presents the images, ideas, and belief systems that a society holds. They have worked their way into what we read, what we care about the way we raise our children and our ideas of right and wrong.

Advertising is a social practice so the expression of sexuality continues to be an issue of social concern. Sex has spread throughout our entire society and has shown that there are very few limits.

The use of sex is most effective for those products that are consumed primarily by younger men. "Advertisements aimed at young male consumers will continue to become more explicit. Advertisers and agency executives say that they have to use graphic, sexually charged images to capture the attention of the consumer and to attract buyers who are bombarded by hundreds of product promotions every day". Like most consumers, males see numerous ads every day in all forms of media and it is generally accepted that explicit sexual images will get men's attention. Most advertising executives think that "sex appeal is the most powerful weapon in their arsenal" and they will have to use even more graphic images to hold on to their audience. Sex provides an effective way of getting men's attention but it's a cheap shot. Advertisers attempt to blur the distinction between women's bodies and the product.

The increasingly graphic sexual images are not aimed only at young men. Sex is also used to sell a variety of products to women. Attractive male models are explicitly displayed as sex objects just as women are. An example of this is a Jeans commercial, which shows a bare-chested, muscular man painting on the walls as the sexy bait for a female living on the street. Another use is in perfume and personal care product ads that appear in women's magazines. The common thread linking most products, which are promoted with sexual images, is that their use affects relations between the sexes and their perceptions of one another.

Perfume by definition is a sexual product, so there is a certain license to sell it that way but these ads implant unrealistic expectations in consumers about their bodies and relations between the sexes. Sexualized imagery in advertising is viewed as power by young women, power being defined as self efficacy or a personal power enabling-one to control one's own life. It has also been found that a young woman's perception of her body can be changed by just 30 minutes of television viewing. This shows how strongly advertisements can affect society, especially women. There has been a great deal of change in the portrayal of women in advertising. This might be because advertising has a powerful role of depicting women not necessarily how they actually behave, but rather, how society thinks women behave. This depiction serves the social purpose of convincing society that this is how women are or want to be, or should be. It seems that only superficial cultural alternations are transferred to advertisements, while the underlying ideological foundation remains untouched.

According to early work, physical attractiveness elicits positive emotional responses during-initial contacts. Attractive persons are typically rated as more desirable, socially acceptable, respectable, and influential than their less attractive counterparts. The physical attractiveness of a communicator determines the effectiveness of persuasive communication, and ultimately, physical attractiveness of the communicator influences overall marketing outcomes. Nudity and erotic content will increase a consumer's attention to an ad, but it won't necessarily enhance positive attitudes toward the product. Attractive spokespersons create a more positive attitude toward ads in hope to give the consumer the impression that it is an attractive product. The past decade has seen intensification in the pace of sexual revolution. Print ads appearing in popular general interest magazines seem to push the limits of eroticism and nudity for both male and female models. Some of these bounds that are being pushed: even include sexually intimate images between models of the same gender. An example of this is a Calvin Klein ad, where two half-naked men embrace one another.

Advertisers must exercise caution when using sex appeals to target their consumers. Any misuse of advertising appeals could prove to be financially costly. Advertising reflects a predominant form of socio-cultural reality from a marketing perspective, it is also important for commercial messages to be socially sensitive and culturally desirable. Advertisers assume that their clients know that consumers are not looking for realism in advertising. They believe that instead the consumer identifies with an idealized depiction of themselves and their sexuality–a fantasy. Advertisers are leaders and not followers, and they often prey on consumers' sexual insecurities. Regardless of the purity and morality of their motives, it is clear that advertisers will continue to find sex as a marketing tool simply irresistible.

If we allow this sexually explicate advertising to continue, eventually it will shape our society into becoming what is being portrayed. Since advertising affects a societies belief system, seeing such things will alter our views and values. If we continue to ignore these vile depictions or let ourselves become used to them, they will only become more extreme in order to catch our attention.

To keep this from happening we could use various tactics. We could not allow ourselves to buy products that use sexually appealing methods. If enough people do this, the company will get the hint that their advertisements aren't working so they will search for a new plan to sell their product. Another way is to create more regulations so that there is a much defined limit to what advertisers can and cannot do and use. We could also protest the companies that use advertisements that we do not approve of. This would cause the company to get bad publicity and for their sales to drop. After this they most likely would change their advertising plans. Selling sex is the most predominant and useful-way to sell a product in today's society. Whether consumers realize it or not, most of the time we are simply buying sex. It is clear that changes in social perception and acceptance about explicit expressions of sexuality with both genders have occurred during the past decade. Advertisers will continue to make advertisements more explicit to catch its audience's attention if changes aren't made. If we disregard or don't pay attention to the increasingly sexual depictions in advertising, it will become predominately worse. To stop more sexual images from appearing in advertisements, society as a whole must take a stand and voice its opinions.

Sex in Media

Television: A Language We Learn to Read

Watching television has become a major part of today's culture, whose people spend an average of three to six hours a day staring at the flickering images transmitted right into their/our living rooms. Still, watching the television has often been seen as a routine, unproblematic, passive process: the meanings of the programme are given as seen and obvious, the viewer is seen as passively receptive and mindless. This would mean, that the television audience does not have to do anything but sit and stare without thinking, and that the pictures we see do not leave any space for interpretation.

This, in fact, is not true. It might just be that we have all grown up learning to interpret the conventions of television in order to put a meaning to the images shown and therefore regard the process of 'reading television' as natural. As we have to learn the alphabet and language to be able to read a book, we also have to learn to interpret images shown on TV to be able to understand them. We constantly have to refer to our knowledge and experience both of the world we live in and the television reality as well. We have to have a certain amount of cultural competence and social knowledge and on the other hand, we have to be familiar with the conventions and requirements of the medium and genre itself.

Television is an oral and visual medium, but, just as in everyday life, we do not consider oral language as highly as the written word. This be because of the long tradition of written text, but this has something to do with the realization that we cannot capture television, which is like an endless flow, a continuous stream going on and on; we just tune in and become part of an impersonal, silent and invisible audience. When reading a book the pace is ours, we can read a sentence over and over again, it will always be there, it is material and gives us a feeling of truth and eternity. Television on the other hand, seems to be transitory and it does not have a beginning and a conclusion, even though the programmers shown on television have. But they are only segments of the whole and not even commercial breaks can take away this assumption of the "endless flow".

Nevertheless, we should not mistake an oral medium to be an illiterate one. After all, television is our window to the world and it uses codes, which are closely related to those by which we perceive reality. As television has quite a huge impact on society and influencing everyday reality, it is itself a human construct, merely reflecting the world it is produced in, presenting its values, morals and ideology (for example gender roles, justice or war coverage), very often favouring the purposes of the authorities, might they be political or industrial.

The media is conceptualized as telling the viewer what to think about or what not to think, or talk about. In watching television, people are persuaded to accept a view of society and of their place in it, that confirms their subordination. The influence of the society is represented in the media on society and culture should not be underestimated, referring to Marshall McLuhan's idea of the global village, which due to globalization becomes more and more of a western community strongly influenced by American values and ideology. Still it goes against the idea of 'active viewer', who has the knowledge and the competence to interpret television in his/her own way, able to turn the set-off when it does not fulfill his/her expectations. Human sense, the cultural environment we live in, our rules and values and our very own personality as well as the viewers' purposes, needs and moods influence the sensory data as well as the context of the programme.

In order to make sense of the world we live in and the world shown to us on TV, we make the use of schemata, we categorize to go beyond the information given, to put meaning to what we observe. Television programmes can be divided into genres, which the viewer recognizes by interpreting conventional signs and codes. There are physical (what we can see) and conceptual (what it means) signifies. And the more often a sign is used, more conventional it becomes, leading the viewer's expectation. The relationship is purely conventional-dependent on social and cultural conventions. Signs themselves depend both on the producer as well as on the audience and different symbols have different meanings in different cultures.

In Semiotics, the science of signs, there are two central concerns: The relationship between a sign and its meaning and the what signs are combined into codes. Signs frequently used in television programmes can be categorized into social, technical and representational codes. Social codes include the dress, the make-up, gestures and language of a character, codes to inform the viewer about the social class of a person, profession and/or education.

Stereotypes are often used because they do not need much explanation and the viewers' expectation, resulting from what he/she has experienced on TV and in his/her own social surrounding, are predictable and can either be fulfilled or broken.

Technical codes, such as the camera, the lighting, the editing or the use of sound and music, also lead to strong expectations and mainly signify the genre of a programme, if it is documentary or drama, fact or fiction, a game show or the news. They also have a strong influence on the mood of the spectators, drawing the audience into the programme, to have them feel what the producer or director intents.

More subconsciously works the lighting of characters, for example, whether a character's face is lit from top or below giving him/her a harsh expression. The camera angle would be another example, while a top shot represents inferiority, vulnerability and insecurity, a low angle lets the character grow, making him superior and strong. Again, technical codes tell the viewer what to expect.

Thirdly, there are Representational codes. The dialogue and the narrative differ from genre to genie. They indicate, for example, whether it is a news-programme we are watching or a comedy. After all, we have learnt these conventions a long time ago and are constantly confronted by them while watching television. And due to our experience, we are able to understand them in a way they are intended to.

Even if we do not understand the actual language of a programme, we can still read the language of television and can judge by interpreting conventional signs and codes. And yet seemingly most obvious conventions, like first showing a person looking at a point off-camera and then showing an object, which we all interpret as this person seeing that object, does not necessarily have to make sense to a viewer who has never experienced television before.

Categorization is a key "top-down" process, which is involved in perception, it helps us to simplify, speeding up our recognition and the procession relation given information to our experiences. If we would not have learnt to read television, we could not understand it. On the other hand, the way we put meaning to what we see on TV does not differ too much in the way we see world we live in anyway.

We perceive both of them, reality and television reality in a similar way and as a result, they interact with each other. Still we have to be and are aware of television framing reality. We understand that television does not only pretend to be realistic, connecting with the experience of the viewer, but also purely entertaining, fitting with the conventions and requirements of the medium and the genre.

Codes, after all, depend on the agreement of the users and therefore are not static but changeable. Conventions nowadays are very different from those fifty years ago. They depend on changes in society, to meet the changing needs and practices of the users. Because we live in a 'different society' nowadays and have the knowledge of the past as well as the present, we cannot relate the given information to our own experience and therefore have a distant look at it. And especially the vision has changed: the speed of images is steadily increasing, but we somehow still seem to manage this huge amount of information. We are used to it, and when people in the future look at today's TV-programmers, they will probably start laughing.

But signs do not vary in time but very much in place, for although a signifier remains the same, the sign itself is altered by change of genre within the medium, as the same way as it is by a change of medium itself. So, to make a meaning out what we see, we have to not only identify the sign but also the genre, referring to the context of the programme, identifying the codes.

Reading television is indeed a very complex process that we seem to achieve effortlessly. As many things in real life, they might be simple to carry out but never simple to analyse. And when breaking down this endless flow of television, we deal with segments that can be read in different ways by the viewers. Because television is a mass medium, most of the programmers are designed to reach as many people as possible and therefore, regarding the differences in social and educational, have to respond on a rather 'low level' to attract as many viewers as possible. Due to changes in transmission, broadcasting is changing into 'narrow casting', which might lead to a development in quiality, but it takes away the event-character of television programmers and would in a way, destroy McLuhan's idea of the 'global village', for it would feed different information.

How we make a meaning of what we see on television is our capability to distinguish between fact and fiction because in real life, what we see is what is true, we primarily trust our sight, even though of course, our experience, our schemata, our knowledge, therefore our perception. But we know that television is 'lying', making up stories, often driven by sensationalism due to a growing competition. Perceiving television might include a lot of modes in which we make sense of our own reality, but in real life, there are not as many signs and symbols, in real life we have to be selective. By no means could have we pay attention to every car passenger passing us on the road, but we learn what things are important, how to interpret them and so on. Television is even faster, there is nothing in the frame that is not supposed to be there, that has a meaning and sometimes the frame is so full of symbols that we only perceive them sub-consciously, we have to decide what data is actually necessary.

There is a danger in television as a medium. Because perception is so close to reality and television can provide the viewer with a multitude of feelings and experiences, we are endangered to make 'TV reality' our reality, to have lives our lives. This will never lead to satisfaction, but it gives the viewer pleasure and a glimpse of happiness. To conclude, 'Televisual' codes constitute a kind of language and we all learn how to interpret signs and symbols in order to put meaning to what we see. This process is oral and visual and does not differ from what we do in perceiving reality in real life very much. Due to differences in cultural and social background all over the world we are likely to interpret the same symbols differently, depending on whatever convention a society has agreed on. But just as well, television is its own medium/mode of communication and therefore obeys its own rules, which we have to take into consideration when figuring out meanings.

It should also be considered that people watch television for different reasons, to actually learn something, experience something or just as background sound in the next room. This again has an effect on how we read television.

Sex in Television

Through the years, sex has grown dramatically on television. Sex has become an open topic on television sitcoms, as a result, sex is amongst the biggest attractions on television. It has become the centre of our most attractive television shows and the whole concept revolves around it. As sex continues to grow on television, so do the viewers.

The sitcom Friends involves middle-aged adults who use sex as an open issue on their show. As sex continues to become more open on these shows, their ratings continue to grow. These types of shows continue to take over our televisions, but others can argue the other side of this issue as well.

As sex draws the recognition of the majority of our viewing audience, there are some television shows that are moving in a different direction. For example, the Star Plus show, *Kaun Banega Crorepati* held the Number One spot among television shows for several months. This fact alone supports the other side of the issue. *Kaun Banega Crorepati* has been by far the most watched programme in Prime Time Television, drawing in million of viewers. So we can see here that there is one thing that attracts people more than sex, Money!

As time goes by, television broadens its horizons and opens up new doors. Television draws in audiences by portraying what's on people's minds and what's going on around them. People will continue to be attracted to money and sex on television because...Sex Sells!

Many commercials aired on television today incorporate sex appeal in the message. Examples include, vacation promotions, liquor, bathroom fittings and even mineral water. But the reactions to such commercials and their acceptance vary from people to people.

Sexual advertising is viewed acceptable because it encourages awareness of the products and in some cases increases the desire for the product. On the other hand, viewers also feel that using sex appeal to sell a product is not acceptable. Viewers and members of the broadcast industry such as executives of these TV channels feel that the use of sex in television commercials is in bad taste and should not be aired.

Today, television commercials cover a wide spectrum of topics. In order to grab the attention of the viewer, advertisers must appeal to some human aspect whether it is humor, emotion or sex. By using sex as the appeal, advertisers run the risk of offending viewers while at the same time accomplishing the goal of getting the attention of the other viewers. There are many examples of sex in television commercials that range from showing bare skinned people, showing sexual movements, gestures and words.

Those in opposition to using sex in commercials have argued that ratings have become necessity for television programmers, yet there are some problems with the rating system. The current plan leaves news, psuedo-news, promos, commercials, sports and other shows that are unrated and warning free. They are often worse than prime time programmers. Those that feel that sex in advertising is acceptable say that sex in advertising can be relevant because it has to have a function and really sell a product. Sexual advertising tries to aid in sales by making the product more desirable.

Sexual Advertising in Magazines

Magazines contain many types of print advertising used to sell products in specified target markets. The print advertising in magazines faces a controversial issue of whether sexual advertising is offensive to the general public. Sexual images have been used to sell products for decades. The question remains as to whether it is wrong to use sex as a selling tool or not.

Sexual images can be used to appeal to the consumer of almost any product. Some of the sexual advertisements in magazines are subtle, while others are blatant. It is clear that sex is a strong appeal to sell certain products, such as fragrance. The use of sexual advertising is prominent in advertisements for fragrances such as Escape, Obsession and Hugo. This advertising is directed at men as well as women.

Products such as shampoo, cosmetics and toiletries are advertised by using seductive women. Also a number of advertisements for apparel designers and manufacturers have also used an element of sex like Calvin Klein, Monte Carlo, Vivaldi, OCM and Grasim suitings or Calvin Klein dealt with the issue of using youth in provocative print ads. The ads were eventually pulled due to their content regarding minors. However the issue of sexual advertising was under scrutiny as a whole. Sexual advertising is questioned even if it does not use under age models. It is questioned because it is considered degrading, immoral or simply offensive.

The use of sexual advertising applies to all forms of print media, so does this type of media really need to use sex appeal to sell the product? The answer is no for there are many products in the same or similar product categories that do not use sexual advertising to sell.

For example if we consider two apparel manufacturers namely, OCM and Raymond's, both have the same kind of product and while OCM uses sexual advertising, Raymond's uses emotions in its advertising but while the Raymond's ads are quite memorable, the OCM ads are nothing to write home about!

Female Role Portrayals in Women's Magazines

Assaulted by criticism from feminist leaders against this presentation of women in advertising, Britain's National Advertising Review Board established a panel to address charges that advertising was rampantly sexist in the 1970s. Women were often portrayed as housewives and too infrequently as professionals. Women were featured as sex objects to the exclusion of their individuality and portrayed often as dependent, requiring men to solve their problems.

Until very recently, Indian magazine advertisements continued to portray women in their stereotypical images. A woman was either shown in the kitchen cooking food, washing a bucketful of clothes, bandaging wounds or feeding her husband and children. Therefore, the picture that emerged was that of a woman who never produced knowledge or wealth but always consumed and remained a sort of hanger-on to her male.

The status of women in India has raised many a controversy and headed many a movement. With the passage of time, the Indian woman's role has metamorphosed from a domestic manager to a prime purchaser. She has now emerged as a potential consumer, ready to redefine her status in the worldwide economy, and her contribution to the society is no longer confined to being solely a progenitor.

Emergence of Women as Consumers

Traditionally, the role of wife and mother has been seen as a woman's destiny and her only career choice. For years, she remained totally dependent on her husband financially and chose to remain unaware of the world outside her home. It was the man who was the consumer for the whole family and thus a target for marketers. However, in the last 40 years, the rapid strides in education and employment have paved the way for drastic changes in the status of women—the latter have become self-reliant and also share enhanced emotional bonds with their husbands.

From the woman confined to the domestic sphere to the liberated woman of the 21st century, from the woman totally dependent on a man to the total independent career woman of today, women have made their way through and have evolved as individuals in their own right. And as far as the notion of consumers is concerned, women have become the target market for products and services in India.

Gender in Advertising

Advertising seems to be obsessed with gender and sexuality and continues to represent an arena in which gender display plays a major role. It has emerged as a world of 'commercial realism' in which we are given 'realistic' images of domestic life and male-female relationships which are not actually real but which provide us with a 'stimulated slice of life'. As gender representation is such a dominant feature of modern day advertising, it is often called the social resource 'used most' by advertisers. In turn, advertising provides an ideal place to examine the encoding of cultural norms and values in ritualized formats.

Increasing Popularity of Women's Magazines in India

Bearing in mind that India has a very low literacy rate, the trend of magazines as an informative and entertaining medium has comparatively gained enormous popularity among the increasing urban population of India. Magazines in India are regarded as a strategic informational, educational and cultural institution as well as the fifth state of public inquest. They are read for gaining knowledge, for recreation and for equipping oneself with the latest information.

Women's magazines were introduced in the Indian market only after the women's liberation movement. They now reach out to women in both urban and rural societies in India and cater to women in terms of their age, class and role. The market for women's magazines is increasing at such a rapid pace that it is no more flooded only with domestic women's magazines but also with global ones such as Cosmopolitan and Vogue which choose to cater to an elite audience. And the ad agencies that create the advertisements in these magazines strive to promote a sophisticated consumerist culture and encourage the readers to imitate the style, philosophy and format of western magazines and advertisements.

Advertising in Women's Magazines

As advertising vehicles, women's magazines are among the most desirable of publications and are aimed at the sector of the population traditionally more responsible for purchases. The strength of these magazines rests principally on the crucial role of women in the consumption process. The front cover of a magazine is the vehicle by which the consumer distinguishes one magazine from another and serves to label not only the magazine but also the consumer who possesses it. Women's magazines use their front covers as advertisements for themselves. Their cover pictures and names, whether it's Hers, She, Women's World or Women's Era, proclaim that these journals are for women only. The cover shapes the reader's understanding of the material in the inside pages.

Promoting the Sexual Stereotypes of Women in Advertisements

Print advertisements, especially those in magazines, cover booklets and posters can be biased against females when they depict them in a sexually suggestive pose. Often times, the presence of the woman herself has nothing at all to do with the product. Therefore, a gender-biased stereotype against females is illustrated in several ways:

- Women are related to the product through a sexual connection.
- Female roles within an advertisement perpetuate female passivity.
- The preferences and expectations of consumer culture create an atmosphere where the female is objectified.
- Socio-economic factors create conditions where the female can only be powerful in the kitchen or when she is nude.
- Female inferiority is presented as a counterpart to male superiority in an ad.
- Print advertisements are able to provoke, titillate and manipulate human behaviour. Moreover, these forces are important to advertisers because they

convince consumers to purchase a particular product and to keep purchasing the product despite of–or maybe because of–its biased presentation. Advertising is the most powerful semiotic force in modern culture today; it transcends economic markets, social institutions, demographics and various purposes. Advertisers are aware of this power and they use it to their advantage.

The basic purpose of advertising is to show people that the product is of use to them in one way or another. Still, if people accept the product and agree with the imagery, they will purchase the product regardless of the gender-biased connotation. Sex in advertising gets people's attention, but it can also be offensive. Advertisers realize they have a limited 'window of opportunity', which means they must convey their messages very quickly, the advertisements do not have the time or the space to go into detail or explanation of the image without ever the chance of being offensive or appearing unprofessional.

Does Sexual Imagery, Particularly the Portrayal of Female Nudity within an Advertisement, Affect an Advertisement's Overall Success?

The answer is Yes! Usually the print advertisements are effective in buying attitudes and brand name recall when a sexual connection is invented with the product. According to one particularly intriguing study that looked at the effects of sexual stereotyping in advertisements, many behavioural effects resulting from the use of sexual appeal exist, especially when a female sexual connection existed within the advertisement. The experiment was conducted of 181 college students and 206 off-campus persons. One group of subjects saw advertisements with sex role stereotypes and the other without any such stereotypes.

The research question asked the two groups if the use of female role portrayal as sex objects in print advertising had an ability to respond to certain brand names and buying attitudes. Subjects were analyzed by:

- Attitude toward women as liberal or conservative; and
- Various demographic characteristics (sex, marital status, race, college major or occupation).

The results of the experiment found that subjects who saw the female portrayed as a sexual object were more likely to recall the brand name of the product and were more likely of purchase the product because of the appeal of the female sexual connotation. Of the subjects who did not see the female sexual imagery, more were less likely to have a favourable buying attitude.

Additionally, the experiment reveals the incredible semiotic forces behind the female image. Sexual stereotypes in print advertisements increase sales revenue. The experiment supports the popular advertising strategy of using sex, biased or not, to sell a product.

The gender-biased stereotypes against women exist in advertising because a sexual connection is easier to set up for a man than for a woman. Men have minimal criteria for sexual desire; they are concerned with the female body—as long as a female is portrayed in a youthful and healthy pose, she is desirable. Men consider the female image beautiful, since to a male beautiful and sexually attractive are basically indistinguishable from one-another.

Advertisers know that exploiting the female body in advertisements is an effective way to capture a man's attention and spending income. Print advertisements present an ideal image of the female to the male consumer. If the male is able to associate the image of the beautiful, passive and demure woman with the product, then he will eventually buy whatever is being sold.

The ads spend no time discussing the female qualifications for sexual desire—her mere presence is enough. Furthermore, advertising can depict a female image and sell the product on the basis that women desire this particular product in a man. The simple strategy being that it will encourage men to think that the product will improve their masculinity because if they obtain the product being advertised they will attract women.

Advertisers use female sexual appeal as an effective strategy, sometimes the exploitation and perpetuation of the female stereotype will lead to quick and profitable revenues. Advertisers will employ these mechanisms whenever sales revenues fail to meet annual expectations for profitable economic gains.

Certain messages about authority and dominance of males are implied through features such as the arrangement of characters, visual and body orientation and other cues that are only indirectly related to the product being advertised. The product relation element within the ads is all but forgotten, much to the dismay of advertisers and to the consumers wanting the product.

Furthermore, it is possible to argue that the public acknowledges messages such as nude imagery, even subconsciously. The public may see the superficial image and it may subsequently be incorporated into an individual's perception of the world including their personal perceptions.

Do Advertisers Ignore Female Buying Attitudes?

No. Mitigating the instinctive view is the intellectual; most buyers of popular products are less concerned with the female anatomy. The use of sex in advertising to women is a more difficult obstacle that advertisers must confront when they use a strategy to sell a product. Sexual desire for women is much more complex and includes more requirements and expectations, most of which are extremely difficult to place in an advertisement within the limited 'window of opportunity' that is available. There are constraints, the most important being the socio-economic attitudes of consumers and the reaction to those attitudes by the advertisers.

The female regards the stereotypes of men to be mainly about career skills, strength and long-term stability in the form of marriage. The male stereotypes in the advertisements must portray his ability to father children, nurture the female during pregnancy and assure that their child will be better off then any other potential male competitors.

Cultural expectations also play a very crucial role in promoting the sexual stereotypes in advertising, they include, but are not limited to: money, power, prestige and fertility. Women expect these abilities in a male through reinforcements that we see in advertising stereotypes and those stereotypes determine her criteria for the sexual desirability of males.

These factors are impossible to put in any one advertisement; there is not enough time or space to set up the appeal and successfully sell the product. Thus, it is rare for print advertisements to promote any gender biased stereotype and sexual appeal when they are marketing the product to women.

Again the limited 'window of opportunity' is a constraint any advertiser must confront, because advertising cannot take advantage of a woman's instinctive sexual desire. Therefore, the purposes of advertisements are not to create gender equality, but sell the product, even if it means that they must reinforce the gender-biased stereotypes of females by exploiting their sexual appeal.

So What is the Socially Acceptable Way to Target a Female Demographic?

To sell to a woman, advertising relies on the modern idea about how men and women relate romance. Romance fits into the woman's intellectual view of relationships since its major element, courtship, the process by which men apply to be and the process that women use for selecting mates, is the discovery of how the male does or does not satisfy her societal criteria for a suitable male sexual partner. Rarely does the romantic appeal contain the blatant sexual messages that appear in ads aimed at men since such messages would counter the intellectual view. Although an ad may use a man's body as an attention-getting device, he is usually shown in a romantic rather than sexual context.

Thus, it becomes clear to advertisers that the use of sex appeal in advertising sells more easily to men than it does to females. Yet, in the cultural world, which often subordinates biology to intellect, this dichotomy between males and female views of sexual appeal can cause a major difference in gender-biases and the perception of a female as being inferior in comparison to male gender superiority.

Advertisements perpetuate gender-biased stereotypes of women in society. Nevertheless, all advertisements are surreal in a sense; they connect disparate objects in strange formal systems and even place familiar products in locations in which they have no obvious connection to the female. Advertising is a diverse and complex field, yet, beneath the gender-biases and stereotypes lies the remarkable simplicity and depth for gender equality—equality without a face value with ideals, values, love and vitality.

Gender equality can be achieved without a sexual connection. This possibility for equality is never permitted to last. Instead, we see sexual biases presented through semiotic symbols, images and idealized concepts. It is within that subtle message that consumers have a cue to create a relationship between ourselves and unobtainable images of beauty and perfection.

The ultimate lesson is that 'Beauty lies in the eyes of the beholder, but do not accept the beauty at face value because it is obtained at a price'. The price we pay is realized through the reinforcement of gender-biased female stereotypes. For example, those features unique to female advertisements, such as sexually implicit cues and suggestive glances convey messages and images that strengthen a negative gender bias stereotype of softness, predictability, laziness or passivity.

It is typical for advertisements to show a male being portrayed as dominant, except in the spaces reserved for women: in the domestic situation or scantily clad. We accept these images sub-consciously or passively because the images portrayed in the print advertisements provide the foundations for future perceptions of a female's position in society. It is a position that we cannot afford to take at face value. Instead, consumers should attempt to change their attitudes and acceptance of these negative female images in advertisements and they should demand to see ads that do not focus exclusively on the sexual appeal.

For many categories, for example, liquor, there is a category mythology, which largely shapes the communication and therefore the brand mythologies:

Liquor = Women and Wine = Separates the men from the boys = Social drink = Loosener =Addictive.

The communication largely echoes the category mythology and uses sexual imageries and archetypes to build that aura of a macho self-confident man who knows what he wants. Tilsbury, Whitehall commercials are clear examples in this category.

Also, advertisers create stereotypes that will appeal to the opposite gender's needs and desires. Attributes that appeal to male stereotypes include power, prestige, good health, longevity, sex and new experiences. Attributes that appeal to female stereotypes include comfort, family, affection, tenderness, fear, romance, generosity and sensory pleasure. Advertisers, therefore, use actors or actresses who can trigger an emotional response from one of the above-mentioned attributes, encouraging the consumer to buy the product.

In the average home, women are the purchasers of household products, such as food and drinks or soaps and shampoos, therefore advertisements for these products target women. Although sexually oriented advertisements aimed to women do not occur as often as they do for men, they are increasing in numbers and popularity.

The use of sex is the most effective for those products that are consumed primarily by younger men. Advertisements aimed at young male consumers will continue to become more explicit. Advertisers and Agency executives say that they have to use graphic; sexually charged images to capture the attention of the consumer.

Category 1: Health Drinks

The product category being health drinks, the largest segments are the young adults and teenagers as these are impulse purchases and the majority of consumption happens but of home. This probably explains the use of sexual innuendoes and spoofs to grab the attention of the viewers.

Description

- The Maaza commercial plays on 'Real Juice' aspect. The commercial opens with a good-looking babe entering a party and all the guys drooling over her. She ignores all the good-looking guys and makes a beeline for a guy who looks like a nerd. The nerd who is holding a Maaza bottle in his hand is absolutely taken aback and waits with a baited breath. The babe comes up to him takes the Maaza and finishes it off, she the wipes his misled spectacles with her dress and walks off. The background music builds the mood and ends with 'You've got the juice', the implication being on the sexual potency and strength.

- Milkman on the other hand harps on the energy giving properties of milk by showing two boys relaxing in the swimming pool when one girl requests them to help her with her suntan lotion. The boys are very eager and try to get out of the pool. The boy who was having the Milkman was immediately able to hop out while the other cannot come out and hence misses on the opportunity. The commercial ends with the Milkman boy gloating on his success and saying *doodh nahin piyega to aisa hi hoga*.
- The Diet Coke commercial highlights the 'one-calorie'. The commercial opens with group of girls playing next to the swimming pool. They are tossing the Diet Coke can to each other at various angles, which highlight the various parts of their bodies. The commercial ends with the slogan, 'feel the power of one'.

Communication Analysis

The communication tends to bring out the fact that Maaza has real juice in it while the Milkman commercial highlights the energy giving properties of milk. The communication of Diet Coke is largely feature based and uses images of active and fit women to highlight the fact that it helps you enjoy Coke without bothering about the calories.

Category 2: Mineral Water

The product category, Mineral water, at first glance seems innocuous enough and somewhat distant for sexual imagery to impact market share. Bisleri, however, has used sexual imagery in their communication.

Description

Bisleri commercial opens up with a couple having fun out in the open. The couple is about to start making love when the woman requests for something. The man tries to find it in their car but cannot and hence drives to a chemist. He gets out and asks for it the chemist hand's him an unbranded box which he carries back to the woman and opens it to reveal Bisleri bottles. The woman enjoys a good swig from the bottle and then they continue their lovemaking. The entire commercial is based on 'Play Safe'.

The Bisleri commercial plays, largely, on the 'safe' aspect when the ad makes the audience feel that the guy is looking for a condom rather than a Bisleri bottle. The music and the treatment of the ad are black & white with the only colours being the blue of the Bisleri and the red of the chemist.

The print campaign for Bisleri shows a compartment with a lot of people, in which TV is on and a couple is kissing on screen, this kiss is hidden behind a pole.

Aquafina, a mineral water launched by Pepsi, used various models dancing to a peppy number while the Ad supers discussed the quantity of water in our bodies.

The models, of both sexes, are of course wearing the bare minimum.

Description

In the Bisleri ad, the use of sex is irrelevant to the product and the only thing that the advertisement stresses on is that Bisleri is safe so if you believe in playing safe in other aspects of life, you should do so while consuming water as well.

Aquafina, just like Pepsi, has tried to connect with the youth, projecting Aquafina as the water of the young and well bodied.

Communication Analysis

The irrelevance of the sexual imagery for a low involvement category like mineral water leaves the consumer high and dry.

Also the consumer is not able to take out anything from the depiction apart from the sale aspect in Bisleri's case.

Category 3: Perfumes and Deodorants

The category of perfumes and deodorants is of high involvement and relies heavily on a sense of self-perception and social acceptance. People use such products to not only get rid of the body odour but also to make oneself, attractive to the opposite sex.

Description

Axe Deodorants commercials have used the sex appeal in all their TVCs and print campaign. One commercial open up with a stylish hunk changing clothes in an elevator and using the Axe deodorant amply. A nerdish looking guy then occupies this elevator and a woman taking the same elevator cannot resist the temptation and goes for the Stop Button. The next shot shows both of them straightening up as the doors open and another woman peeps in admiringly at the guy.

Another TVC has a man after quitting a job, takes out Axe bottle like a lethal weapon and sprays himself and walks out. He attracts women like the Pied Piper of Hamlin attracted mice and women from various walks of life let go of their works to follow him.

The Print campaigns, simply reiterate the Axe Effect by showing a Nun with a Clip on her nose, a wedding cake with a number of plastic/wax brides climbing the levels reach the Bride n Groom on the top, a Screw nail in the centre surrounded a number of nuts etc.

Hugo perfumes has a whole campaign with the punch line–'Make your own Rules'. One of them shows a couple in bed biting each other, all over their bodies with the voice over saying 'Don't Eat between Meals'.

Another commercial shows a girl sitting on a couch throwing light on a guy sleeping on the bed in order to wake him up while the voice over states "Wait for him to make the First move?" as the guy wakes up the girl gets up from the couch.

Obsession perfume shows the bare back of a woman sitting in a bathroom.

Depiction

Axe Deodorants have used the need for social acceptance and taken it to a new high by projecting the Axe users as simply irresistible.

Hugo Red, targeting the women, tries to show that by wearing this perfume, one can live their life, the way they want it!

Obsession perfume ad shows that it is meant for those who take desires to an obsessive levels.

Communication Analysis

Perfumes and Deodorants are products that rely heavily on an Emotional cognition. Hence Axe does well by communicating to their target group of the youth, the Axe effect that makes them irresistible.

But both Obsession and Hugo fail to form such a connection with the audience by the use of sexual appeal.

Category 4: Bathroom Fittings

The Product category of bathroom fittings like faucets, showers etc. is a low involvement category with a limited amount of emotional association possible yet Jaguar has used an element of sex in their advertising.

Description

The TV commercial opens up with a woman bathing with a hand shower in a bathroom while her husband waits outside. She moans out of pleasure. The husband starts pacing up and down the room curious as to what she is up to. After she comes out of the bathroom, he goes into investigate and accidentally turns on the shower. Final shot shows the woman hearing her husband's moans.

Depiction and Communication Analysis

The commercial has attempted to relate the pleasure of taking a bath with Jaguar showers to the act of making love.

But the use of moans to imply the sexual act does not go well with the audiences and does not motivate one to upgrade the product usage from one of necessity to that of sensory gratification.

Category 8: Beauty Products (Hair Colorants, Aftershaves, Hairgels Shaving Creams)

Hair dyes and sex? It is an odd combination but it has been used by Sunsilk Procolor. It is High Involvement category, which depends largely on the formation of an emotional cognition. Emami Shaving Cream, Brylcream and Denim Aftershaves also use an element of sex to appeal to their audiences.

Description

Sunsilk Procolor commercial opens up with Close-up of a young girl contemplating whether it would be alright to do it or not since it was her first time and she wanted to be sure that it was going to be safe and ensure that her parents would object etc. Then she gives a go-ahead to Jawed Habib to colour her hair.

Emami Shaving Cream commercial opens with a shot of a woman blindfolding a guy while they lie on a bed and then she smears his face with the cream and shaves it off with a razor.

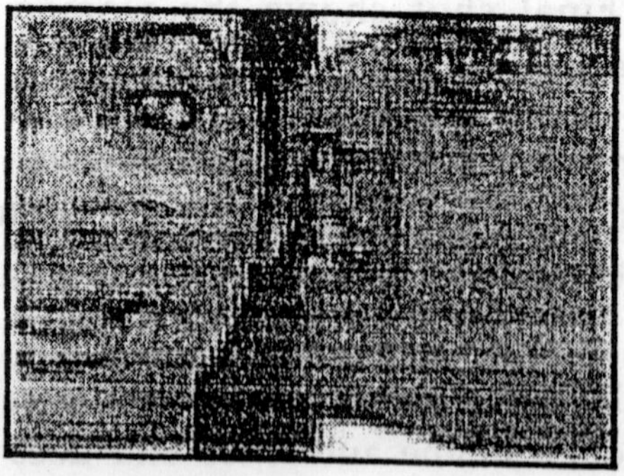

Denim man is the one who doesn't have to try too hard. So the commercial opens with a man walking into an airport checking and a woman cop feels him up and finally puts handcuffs on him.

Brylcreem commercial opens up with a guy clad only in a towel in his bathroom trying on various hairstyles and getting ratings 0-10 from the three women standing in a balcony opposite his house. He gets mild responses from them for each hairstyle till in the end he takes-off his towel and one of the women shows him her telephone number, the commercial ends with the ringing of a phone and a woman answering in a seductive voice.

Depiction

The Sunsilk Procolor commercial tries to portray the decision of colouring one's hair being as tough as one to lose virginity, but with a product like Sunsilk Procolor this decision becomes quite easy.

Emami, Denim and Brylcreem commercials show that using their products will make men attractive to women.

Communication Analysis

The Sunsilk Procolor commercial tries to answer the apprehensions and queries related with coloring one's hair–a concept relatively new in India and succeeds in communicating this to the target audience.

Emami, Denim and Brylcreem commercials try to relate to the basic need of men to look good to attract the opposite sex and the ads hints at the fulfillment of this desire by the usage of these products.

Category 6: Dotcoms

The category is essentially of a service rather than a product. But although a number of Dotcoms advertise on TV, only Baaze.com has used an element of sex in it's advertising although it is completely irrelevant to the brand.

Description

The commercial opens with an elderly couple trying to eat dinner while they can hear noises from their neighbour's house. They can hear a couple screaming-Higher, Higher etc. the next shot shows the other couple actually bidding on Baaze.com. As they finish one bid, the elderly couple next doors start having dinner again but then the younger couple starts another bidding and the elderly man shakes his head in disbelief and frustration.

Depiction

The commercial compares the act of bidding and love-making. It shows that bidding on Baaze.com is just as exciting as having sex.

Communication Analysis

The commercial fails to convey any information regarding except that it is exciting.

Category 7: Shoes

The product category of shoes is a High involvement-highly emotional category whereby people select shoes that go with their personality apart from providing comfort. Red Tape and Reebok shoes to appeal to their target audience of affluent and stylish males have used as an element of sex.

Description

The Red Tape commercial opens with a shot of a woman reaching out for a guy whom she throws on the bed and precedes to undress. Just then, the bell rings and its her husband. So she asks the guy to leave. Her husband walks into the room and sees this pair of shoes, which he tries on and keeps them in a cabinet while complaining that his wife always brought him shoes that never fit.

The Print campaign for Reebok shoes shows a picture of a naked woman clad just in Reebok shoes. But to maintain the last vestiges of censors and refrain from pornography, they have converted the picture into a collage of sorts—of various body parts. Although, the same concept was tried by Tuff shoes in India, it resulted in a ban on the ad and a huge dispopularity of the brand.

Depiction

Stylish guys who do not live by the social rules and act immorally wear Red Tape shoes. The Reebok ad seems to ask the Reader: Who needs clothes when you've got Reebok?

Communication Analysis

The ad does not communicate the quality of the product or the styles available but simply with an element of humour and sex tries to convey that it's a product for those who live dangerously but in style.

Category 8: Clothing

The category of clothing is very broad and since there are a number of different kind of clothing appealing to and targeted at various different groups, it becomes imperative that we break it up into different Sub-categories of Formal wear or Suitings, Casual wear or Jeans and Undergarments. Formal wear or suitings is a category, which is targeted at executive class, slightly more mature male audience. Although many brands advertise in this category, only two–Vivaldi and Grasim have used an element of sex in their advertising.

Sex has been used since time immemorial in Media and advertising. Even in India, if the use of sex was not that frequent earlier, it has been on the rise with the advent of Satellite Television. With the telecast of various channels and foreign soaps like the Bold and the Beautiful, Santa Barbara and Baywatch and subduing of the raised temper of the vast population which began to take such displays of sexuality on screen in their stride, the use of sex appeal has gained popularity in India. But the Use of Sex still remains like a twin-edged sword. Even when it appeals to your Target Audience, it may cause dissonance amongst other groups which leads to devaluation of Brand Perception and hence Success.

References

"Art of Advertising" by Richard F. Taflinger.

Committee of Advertising Practice. Codes of Practice by Courtney, A., and Whipple, T.

Sex Stereotyping in Advertising. Lexington.

"Product class effects on perceived risk: The role of emotion". International Journal of Research in Marketing, Arjun Chaudhuri.

"An Investigation of Mood Commercials", in Cognitive and Affective Responses to Advertising, Patricia Cafferata and Alice M. Tybout. Lexington.

"The Role of Emotion in Advertising", Psychology and Marketing by Holbrook, Morris B. and John O'Shaughnessy.

"The Rossiter-Percy Grid and Emotional Response to Advertising: An Initial Evaluation", Journal of Advertising Research by Kover, Arthur J. and Joseph Abruzzo "Creativity vs. Effectiveness? An integrating classification for advertising" by Kover, Arthur J., Stephen M. Goldberg and William L. James (1995), Journal of Advertising Communication", Advertising Management by Rajeev Batra, John G. Myers, David A. Aaker.

Advertising and Portrayal of Women

The Eight Classes of Advertising

We now look at eight distinct and particular classes of advertising, each of which calls for a distinct treatment and sometimes different media:

1. Persuasive
2. Informative
3. Institutional
4. Financial
5. Classified
6. Retail
7. Co-operative
8. Industrial.

1. Persuasive Advertising. Persuasive Advertising is also known as "hard sell" advertising, this is the most obvious kind of advertising which surrounds us in our daily live, urging us to buy all manner of products and services. Without such kind of sales promoting advertising it is hard to imagine how modern society with its mass production and mass consumption could survive. Seating comments are made about the "admass", but its critics happen to enjoy the plentiful supply of goods which satisfy their economic needs, food, clothes and shelter. Countless pleasure and former luxuries are also enjoyed simply because economics of scale can be exploited, thanks to advertising and other aides to distribution to national and international markets. The argument for advertising is very much same as the argument for the common market. The alternatives to advertising is to revert to medieval style of life with self-sufficient production and modestly adequate incomes for most craftsman, little commercial intercourse with other towns, innate no banking, no credit and religious antipathy towards money lending and making profits. It is interesting that economic historians have noted the link between capitalism and protestarism. Persuasive Advertising in the inevitable companion of industrialization. There is no point in having machines if markets cannot be found for their output. It is the persuasive advertising that finds the markets and keeps the wheels of industry turning by maintaining demand. But not only machines need advertising. A holiday resort cannot fill its hotel bedrooms, nor can a theatre attract a nightly evidence without advertising.

2. Informative Advertising. A lot of advertisements fall midway between the persuasive and the informative. There are exceptions such as proprietary medicine and treatment advertisements which sell by means of facts, evidence, testimonials and other lengthy copy. Persuasive advertisements tend to appear on TV and in popular press, while informative ones are more likely to appear in magazines or weekend newspapers which are read more thoroughly or in less hurried circumstances. There is also the informative advertising which hardly seems to sell at all, telling us interesting things that are some what removed from the product it self, or creating a mood which makes us feel favourably disposed towards the product. Here we have "soft-sell" as opposed to the "hard-sell" appeal. The tobacco firms are adapt at using this technique, promoting leisure and pleasure activities to associate pleasure with their products.

3. Institutional Advertising. Institutional Advertising is also known as prestige or corporate advertising, this is the type of advertisement are used to present the companies image, as when an oil or pharmaceutical company takes space to describe its research skills its contribution to society or its efforts to combat pollution. In this case advertising techniques and media are being used to perform a PR task. The advantage of using institutional press advertising is that the message can be issued is a precise and controlled fashion on specific dates. Thus, urgency may occur in the throes of a take over bid, or if an industry is threatened with nationalization. Most PR work is rather less urgent, and the effort to establish a corporate image–that is, what the organization does and stands for is usually spread over a conscious and accumulative effort.

4. Financial Advertising. Financial advertising does not have to be sober. In recent years there has been a revolution in financial advertisement. As the banking world has shed some but not all of its inhibitions and traditions of bowler hated conformity. Banks, Unit Trust and Insurance companies have sought users to their services and investors from wider and sometimes younger sections of the public. There are, of course, many traditional forms of financial advertisements such as those required by the stock exchange in the event of a new share issue, and very formal pages of small print, setting out a company's history and prospects, appear in business newspaper. Companies also issue very formal announcements about their trading results, but some go further and offer readers attractively presented information based on annual report and accounts.

Perhaps the chief characteristic of financial advertising is its details. Readers usually want to know a lot about the offer being made, whether it be a unit trust, a life insurance policy, a new share issue. The reader wants to know "what's in it for him." What are the risks and the rewards and what are the safeguards. This calls for meticulously detailed copy, even more so than in the case of the informative or educational advertisement already discussed. The copy has to answer all likely questions and be convincing about it.

5. Classified Advertising. While a great many classifieds are inserted by private individuals, others are placed by commercial firms as well as seen for instance in the vacancy columns of both national newspapers and magazines. There is a special art in writing an almost telegram like ad, in a few lines using an intriguing opening to catch the reader's eye the impact of a classified is lost if the copy is too long.

By classified we mean not only that the advertisement are small run on but they are grouped together under identifying headings such as "HOUSE FOR SALE, OFFICE TOLET, SITUATIONS VACANT

OR EDUCATIONAL" etc. This class of advertising is a very important source of revenue to publishers.

6. Retail Advertising. Obviously, retail advertising has to work very hard, even harder than a persuasive advertisement for a manufacturer. The rewards, or lack of them, will be equally obvious. Such advertising is critical to success and survival of a shopkeeper. Not only does he have to buy skillfully and provide good services to his customers, but he has to understand how to make advertising achieve the four objectives set out about. This task becomes all the more difficult when one considers what little understanding the smaller trader is likely to have of advertising techniques and that his total expenditure probably does not justify the services of an agency. He can, however, take advantage of the service departments of local media. But the second objective, establishing character, demonstrates the use and value of advertising in this field. Whether the advertisements are splashed with the bargain offers or whether they are set out in the sophisticated style.

7. Co-operative Advertising. The four types of co-operative advertising which are as follows:

(i) Co-operative society and agriculture similar co-operative trading organization. This is really only a form of retail advertising and is introduced here merely for the sake of clarifying the succeeding forms.

(ii) Joint advertising placed by a trade association, a national export organization or a publicity committee set up on the behalf of an industry.

(iii) Mutual advertising schemes where two or more firms combine their advertisement as in the cases of fashion houses and departmental stores, bread and butter packaged holidays.

(iv) Dealer support schemes which are also known as co-operative schemes. The manufacturer may either subsidize the stockist's advertising, usually or 50-50 basis or supply free advertising material, such as stock blocks of products or complete stereos or artwork of advertisements, with a space left for the insertion of the dealer's name and address. In these ways, the manufacturer can encourage the dealer to promote the goods while the dealer can obtain assistance from the manufacturer both financially and creatively. However, co-operative dealer schemes are most applicable to consumers durables which are sold through appointed dealers than to mass consumer products which are sold through every available outlet.

8. Industrial Advertising. Most industrial advertising, offer raw materials, components and services to manufacturer and users to convert these technical things into finished product which, in turn, are advertised to the end user or final consumer. A house or a motor car, a TV receiver or a central heating system is an assembly of items made by others. It is sometimes said that a fault of British motor industry is that is comes to a halt if the makers of steel, glass, wheels or engine components goes on strike. Industrial advertising aims to sell, say, plastic rain water, pipes, retreated timber to fill panels, wood block flooring, windows, bricks, roofing

Partner Schools

Kellogg London Business School Wharton

"...I look at my management degree as a shot in the arm for the future"

Dr. Mallika Kapur, MBBS
Class of 2005

"I was trained to be a doctor. However, a career in a pharmaceutical company is a different game altogether.

That's why I'm here on a year's sabbatical. And I chose ISB because it trains people to lead rather than merely manage.

My peer group comes from widely different and interesting backgrounds. The faculty is drawn from the best B-schools worldwide. And for a work intensive course, ISB has all the amenities and the lifestyle values that compare with the best in the world.

I look at it as vitamin fortification for my medical career."

Visit us at www.isb.edu for detailed information on our admission road shows.

ISB

Get future ready

Indian School of Business, Hyderabad-500 019

sites, insulation materials, and so on to house builders. The advertisers are sometimes referred to as secondary suppliers, their promotional activities–often making good of PR techniques such as press relations, documentary films and technical seminars are called back selling. The advertiser has the problem that his product may be seldom or never known to the final customer, and so sales can rarely be achieved by appealing to the final customer for support. The new car has a certain make of battery, tyres, instruments and so on and the buyer has no say in what shall be under the bonnet, on the wheels or on the dashboard. It is only at the replacement stage that the car owner can exercise a choice, and then he may decide to fit his own choice of tyres.

It principal medium for this kind of advertising is the trade and technical press (which also run most of the trade exhibitions).

Portrayal of Women in Advertising

Electronic or print media has a very important role and a responsibility towards a clear and healthy advertising which nowadays rarely we receive in this environment of self-styled world. Women which plays different roles in our society should be portrayed in a very respective manner accordingly. An advertisement of lipstick portrays a women in a very strange manner the chest is exposed in costume where only lips could serve the purpose. The ad of liquor does not require any women model even then to make it an attraction along with men, the women accomplices them although one has never heard women take wine regularly. Never so why the women have shown indulging in promoting liquor, this is absolutely ridiculous. We cannot tolerate these types of ads on TV while watching with family. Its does not entertain a family at all. Generally we witness different type of ads on TV which do not make a good impression on our minds. It is a self-styled world of advertisers, all ads are made to make an impression on consumers mind but it makes a quite different impression which is never acceptable in over conservative society. People have different ways of taking things or reject them.

But portrayal of women in advertising should be done in a very intelligent manner at least the subject must be relevant to the matter. It is not relevant if you want to show the ad of a bra all the times you focus on a semi-nude chest of a women, bra can be show under the clothes–the only motto is to show the bra no need to expose the chest directly.

In an ad of trousers a women is taking off her pant to show her bare legs, no need to show them simply you can show the trousers which is the main product.

Vulgarity in Advertising

This is a very controversial topic and a topic of main attraction for all those who are attached with media or any other field because the focus on women in advertisement needs to be decent and mannerful. On the other hand this serious topic is never taken in a proper manner. Women are portrayed in advertisement in a very vulgar way that you cannot enjoy the ad in front of your family members. Now who is to be blamed? Again a question comes in front of us and seeking a reasonable reply from us that for how long this type of vulgarity will be continue? Since the critics are therein the arena one cannot make fool of them.

Most of the ad companies are carrying so much of sex stuff to show through their advertisement. But it clearly shows that they are not focusing on their target but trying to attract people psychology.

Suppose, you have to advertise for a lipstick you are suppose to show only lips in ad, but besides lips something more is exposed in ads. This is a clear vulgarity and one cannot deny it.

So, vulgarity in advertisement is a never ending process. It requires a lot of efforts to control over it but even the years have passed nothing concrete could be done to control vulgarity in advertising.

Let us take a broad look at few popular advertisements.

L'OREAL Beauty Products

L'Oreal is a world renowned beauty brand which can very well sell by name or a ad which displays the beauty of a woman's face, eyes, lips and many more but need not display women in transparent clothes and giving a clear view of her body as shown in the ad adjacent.

OYZTERBAY Jewellery

This is a jewellery brand which can be displayed very well in the ad by showing the beauty of the ring, necklace or earrings etc. as shown by another beauty brand Nakshatra. The comparison between the brand ads displays that one brand displays the beauty of a woman's face by focussing on her earrings and the other displays the woman in a short dress displaying her legs without any reason.

NIVEA Body Products

Nivea is again a brand which needs no description. The quality of the product speaks on its own but one can't make sense out of the ad in which a women is shown in few clothes addressing her body to be beautiful. Of course one can appreciate the beauty of the body by displaying it maybe even in a saree or any western dress that would show her beauty.

Jadore Perfumes

This is an international brand Christian Paris's product and shows a women in semi-nude posture to advertise for the perfume. This seems really out of way that to display the fragrance they show the model in semi-nude posture.

Evamode Inner Wear

This brand is selling the inner wear for women. Of course the product is such and cannot be advertised without the display of the product but it does not make sense to display the beauty of the product along with a model wearing them. These as the name suggests are inner wear and hence are things of daily usage, concluding that they need not be displayed on someone's body to advertise about them.

Lovable Cotton Essentials

Like the brand we spoke of earlier this brand is clearly and boldly displaying the lady wearing the inner garments plus sensational designs add to the vulgarity in the ad.

TAG Heuer Watch

The advertisement of the watch shows a woman in swimming costume make a dive. The logic of showing a lady in a swimming costume in a watch's ad is not understandable and shows a clear picture of the scenario in advertisement regarding women.

Cosmopolitan Magazine

Cosmopolitan is a very popular magazine and is pretty informative. This magazine considers topics from all norms of life tending more to relationships etc. But this magazine is full of advertisements as well as articles with vulgar pictures. As shown adjacent: Is the cover page of the magazine and one can very well judge the matter it contains.

References

1. Advertisement made simple series by Frank Jefkins.
2. Advertising, Mass Communication in Marketing by C.A. Kirkpatrick.
3. Femina, Cosmopolitan.

6

Impact of Advertising on Rural India

The Rural Market–A Big Task for the Advertisers

The Indian society is a complex social system with different castes, classes, creeds and tribes. The high rate of illiteracy added to the inadequacy of mass media impedes reach almost to 80 per cent of India's population who reside in village.

Indian advertising has yet to shed its elitist urban image and open up the vast rural market which, in per capita terms, may be poor but which in the aggregate, is an important market segment (80 per cent of the Indian population resides in village) to which advertising has not yet spread to the desired extent. Beside this it has a great role to play in assisting in the eradication of poverty, for 46 per cent of our population lives below the poverty line communicating the availability of goods, services and opportunities and in contributing to improvements in living standards. Thus there is a big task for the advertisers to exploit this vast rural market which is still unveiled because bulk of the Indian population resides in villages.

Rural Spending

1. **Agricultural Implements**
   - (i) Pumps
   - (ii) Tubewells
   - (iii) Tractors
2. **Vehicles**
   - (i) Cycles
   - (ii) Two-Wheeler
3. **Means of Entertainment**
   - (i) Transistors
   - (ii) Two-in-ones
   - (iii) TV set
4. **Home Appliances**
   - (i) Gas Ovens
   - (ii) Pressure cookers
   - (iii) Mixers
5. **White Goods**
   - (i) Refrigerators
   - (ii) Coolers
   - (iii) Washing machines

Landmarks in Rural Marketing in India

- **Coke uses are to reach out to rural folks December 4, 2003.** Coca-Cola India has embarked on a plan to cater to the rural population through its rural marketing initiative in Maharashtra. As a part of this initiative, a co-branded musical activity–the

'Thumbs-Up Chowfulla' was recently organized in several districts and villages all over Maharashtra.

- **Rural Network and Liba to Conduct Course in Rural Marketing, November 10, 2003.** The Rural Network and the Management Development Centre of LIBA (Loyola Institute of Business Administration), Chennai have course director is R.V. Rajan, CMD, Anugrah Madison, a promoter member of the Rural Network, an informal alliance of leading players in Rural Marketing viz., Anugrah Madison-Channai, MART-Delhi , Rural Relation Pune and Sampark-Mumbai
- **HLL'S New Rural Initiative to Raise Consumption, July 20, 2002.** Hindustan Lever Ltd (HLL) has planned a rural marketing programmes that world result in a double-digit growth in the consumption of the company's products in the rural market. HLL will adopt a three pronged marketing strategy-new price points, sizes and awareness campaigns-for its detergents and soaps segments to augment rural growth.
- **JK Tyre kicks off aggressive rural marketing programme, June 5, 2002.** JK Tyre has kicked off an aggressive rural marketing programme 'Sahi Chunao' (Right Choice) to bolster tractor tyre sales.
- **Philips to launch, May 7, 2002.** Philips is to launch an integrated rural marketing programme called, "Mahasangram" in the month of June. Philips is doing so in a bid to leverage the time tested FMCG style of distribution.

दीपावली की हार्दिक शुभकामनाएं
किर्लोस्कर
"चैम्पियन"
सबमर्सिबल पम्पस
150 mm एवं 200 mm बोरवेल सबमर्सिबल पम्प
• बिजली की भारी बचत
• पूर्ण संतुलित घूमने वाले पुर्जे.
• स्टेनलेस स्टील स्टेटर ट्यूब के साथ
वोल्टेज रेंज
200 - 440 वोल्ट
दाम भी कम
POWER SAVING
KIRLOSKAR PUMPS
SHAKUN
Kirloskar
किर्लोस्कर ब्रदर्स लिमिटेड
अप्रतिनिधित्व क्षेत्रों से व्यापारिक पूछताछ आमंत्रित है।
एरिया सेल्स एक्जीक्यूटिव : मुरादाबाद : संजय शिंदे, 21, पंचशील कॉलोनी, फोन : 0591-2428030, डीलर : मेरठ : एम.पी. ट्रेडिंग कॉर्पोरेशन, खैर नगर, आजाद मार्केट, फोन : 2528284, 2523531, सहारनपुर : जनक इंजीनियरिंग कंपनी, विक्रम भवन, रेलवे रोड, फोन: 2724523, मित्तल मशीनरीज स्टोर्स, रेलवे रोड, फोन: 2644948, गाजियाबाद : वेस्टर्न इंडिया एजेन्सीज, हापुड़ रोड, फोन : 24730124, 24733056

मुफ्त
रु.10,000/-
तक का
इन्श्योरेन्स
महिन्द्रा के प्रत्येक वाहन की
खरीद पर 10000/- तक का
इन्श्योरेन्स मुफ्त पायें।
आकर्षक ब्याज*
पर ऋण की सुविधा
तुरन्त उपलब्ध.
जल्दी करें!
कही देर न हो जाये।
यह योजना
25 नवम्बर, 03 तक.
महिन्द्रा
●बिजनौर ★तिरुपति आटोमोबाइल्स फो. 01342-
9837083345, 9837098058 ● बुलन्दशहर
लि., 6, राजे बाबू रोड, फो 05732-225129 ● गाजियाबाद
आटोमोबाइल्स, III सी-/98, 2796007
2796225 2796385 9412218966 ●नोयडा आटोमोबाइल्स

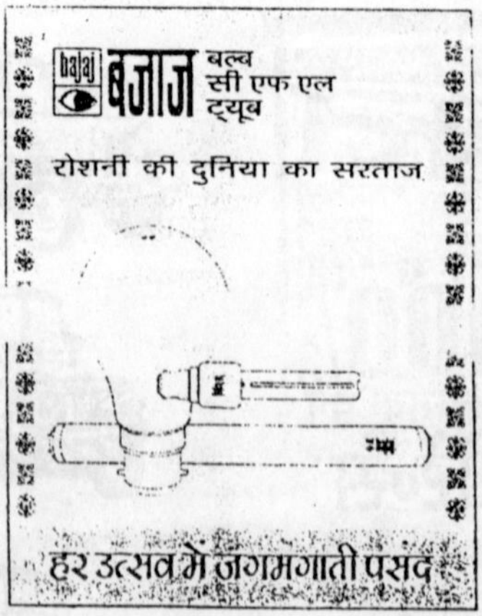

- **RK Swamy BBDO to float healthcare and Social and marketing division April 05, 2002.** R.K. Swamy BBDO will float two new division this year–health care social and rural marketing. The agency has already started operation in both the areas, separate divisions were not floated till now.

- **Department of Post to sell space on postcards for advertisement, March 25, 2002.** The Department of Post has decided to sell one-third space on post-cards for advertisements. The experiment will start with the recently launched "Meghdoot post cards." The focus would be on those companies that are looking for an effective tool for rural marketing.

- **Advertising agencies upbeat as rural marketing becomes mantra for corporate, August 4, 2001.** Advertising agencies like Lowe Lintas and O&M are making the most out of the opportunity, with several FMCG clients looking towards Indian villages to market their products.

Traditional Media and its Importance in Rural Marketing

Mass media is too glamorous, interpersonal and unreliable in contrast with the familiar performance of traditional artist who the villager could not only see and hear but even touch. Besides this villagers are more conservative buyers than their urban counterparts. Their desire to innovate with new product is restricted.

Traditional media can be used to reach these people in the marketing of new concept. The traditional media with its effective reach, powerful input and personalized communication system will help in realizing the goal. Besides this when the advertisement is couched in entertainment it goes down easily with the villager.

Advantages of Traditional Media

- The accessibility is high.
- Involves more than one sense.
- Interest arousal capability is high.
- Less operational liability... minimum cost.

Disadvantages of Traditional Media

- Range of mode choice is narrow.
- Potential for cognitive gain retention is possible but restricted.
- Depends on the skill of the performer. But for optimum effect all elements in the communication system will have to be orcheastered into a united whole.
- Companies like Bajaj, Rajdoot, HLL, Nirma are the few companies which have used these methods to the fullest extent.

Few companies which have used traditional media effectively and the strategy behind it are :

1. *The Strategy:* Dabur address the rural marketing for its Gripewater to both men and women.

   The Lesson: Rural women make the decision. It's the men who buy.

2. *The Strategy:* Reckitt and Colemen uses NGO's in rural areas to educate customers about product benefits.

   The Lesson: Establishes one-to-one communication channels.

3 *The Strategy:* BBLIL markets its rural brands through magic shows and skits.

   The Lesson: Use local idioms to convey your message in a meaningful context.

4. *The Strategy:* Hero Honda has established mobile service centres to take care of rural customers.

   The Lesson: Reinforce product quality through service indicators.

Different Traditional Media Used in Villages

Few of the available options in the traditional media are Puppetry, Folk Theatre and Song, Wall Painting. Demonstration, Posters, Agricultural Games. Postcards, etc.

Puppetry

Puppetry is the indigenous theatre of India. From time immemorial it has been the most popular form and well-appreciated form of entertainment available to the village people. It is an inexpensive activity. The manipulator uses the puppets as a medium to express and communicate ideas, values and social messages.

Types of Puppet Theatre in India

- String puppets or Kathputlis of Rajasthan–

  Contents– Heroic deeds of Vikramaditya, Prithviraj Chouhan. Amar Singh Rathore.

- String puppets of Orissa.

  Contents– Radha-Krishna.

- Rod puppets from Bengal :

  Contents– Mahabharat, Manas, Radha-Krishna.

- String and Rod puppets of the south (Tanjavur, Chennai and Anghra) :

  Contents– Kathakali

- Shadow puppets of (a) Orissa (b) Kerala (c) Andhra (d) Karnataka :

  Contents– Ramayana

Thus in rural India puppetry is a source of livelihood, avenue for entertainment and creative expression which is rituality sacred and meaningful as a means of social communication and vehicle of social transformation.

Song and Drama Division of the Government of India makes wide use of puppets in its campaigns to promote various government projects. Several other organizations, government, semi-government and private, have also used puppets in support of individual schemes.

Life Insurance Corporation of India used puppets to educate rural masses about Life Insurance; enlisting

the help of the literacy house in Lucknow. These plays were shown to the audience in villages in UP, Bihar and MP. The number of inquires at local Life Insurance Companies during the period immediately following the performance was compared with normal frequency and found to be considerable higher. The field staff of the corporation also reported a definite impact on the business.

Indian Institute of Mass Communication, New Delhi made a study of comparative impact of puppetry and documentary films, in two villages near Delhi. People in both the villages responded more favourably to the puppet shown than the films.

Folk Theatre

Folk theatres are mainly short and rhythmic in form. The simple tunes help in informing and educating the people in informal and interesting manner. It has been used as an effective medium for social protest against injustice, exploitation and oppression.

Folk Theatre/ Songs Forms in India

- Andhra Pradesh: Veethi Natakam, Kuchpudi, Burratatha.
- Assam: Ankiya Nat, Kirtania Natak, Ojapali.
- Bihar: Bidesia, Senkela Chhau, Jat-Jatni Bidpada, Ramkhelia.
- Gujarat : Bhavai.
- Haryana : Swang, Naqqal
- Himachal Pradesh : Kariyala, Bhagat, Ras Jhanki, Harnatra Haran or Harin.

- Jammu and Kashmir: Bhand Pathar or Bhand Jashna, Vetal Dhamali.
- Karnataka: Yakshagan, Santa, Doddata-Bayalata, Tala Maddle or Prasang. Dasarata, Radhna.
- Kerala: Kodiyattam, Mudiattam Therayattam. Chavittu Natakam, Chakiyar Kooth, Kathakali.
- Madhya Pradesh: Maanch, Nacha.
- Maharashtra: Tamasha, Lalit Bharud, Gondha, Dashavatar.
- Orissa: Pala Jtra, Daskathia, Chhau Mayurbhanj, Mangal Ras, Sowang.
- Punjab: Nautanki, Naqaal, Swang.
- Rajasthan: Khyal, Rasdhari, Rammat, Turra Kilangi, Gauri, Nautanki, Jhamtara.
- Tamil Nadu: Therukuttu, Veethi Natakam, Bhagwat Mela Natakam, Kurvaanji, Pagal Vasham, Kavadi Chindu.
- Uttar Pradesh: Ram Leea, Ras Leela, Nautanki, Bhagat, Sang-Swang, Naqqual.
- Goa, Daman and Diu : Dashavatar, Tiyatra.

Folk songs have been effectively used during revolts of Telangana and Naxalbari and nowadays it's best exploiters are Political Parties.

Government has used this media for popularizing improved variety of seeds, agricultural implements, fertilizer etc., Punjab Agricultural University produced Two Audio Cassettes.

- Balliye Kanak Biye–Wheat Cultivation.

- Khiran Kepah Narme–Cotton Cultivation.

Both were well received by farmers.

BBLIL used Magician quite effectively for launch of Kadak Chhap Tea in Etawah.

Demonstration

"Direct Contact" is a face to face relationship with people individually and with groups such as the Panchayats and other village groups. Such contact helps in arousing the villager's interest in their own problem and motivating them towards self-development. Demonstration may be

(A) (i) Method demonstration

(ii) Result demonstration

(B) (i) Simple Demonstration

(ii) Composite Demonstration

The five steps to make any demonstration effective are below:

- Information about people
- Objectives to be accomplished
- Demonstration plan and Execution of the plan
- Evaluation of the demonstration
- Reconsideration after evaluation

In result demonstration, help of audio-visual media can add value. Asian Paints launched Utsav range by painting Mukhiya's house or Post Office to demonstrate that paint does not peel off.

Haats and Melas

The countries oldest tradition holds the key to solving these problems. The mobile supermarkets of rural India.

Facts and Figures

- Over 47000 haats and 25000 melas are held annually.
- The average daily sale at a Haat is about Rs. 2025 lacs.
- Annual sales at melas amount to Rs. 3500 crore.
- Over half the shoppers at haats have shopping lists.
- More than 10,000 melas draw visitors from all over India.
- Nearly half the outlets at melas are for manufactured goods.
- Haats is a better opportunity for promotion after brand building has been done at mela.

Melas are organized after harvest season, so the villager has enough money which he will be ready to spend.

Demonstration at Haat is essential to convert customers at haats since their attitude is far more utilitarian than that of visitors to a fair.

Wall Paintings

Wall paintings are an effective and economical medium for advertising in rural areas. They are silent unlike traditional theatre. A speech or film comes to an end, but wall painting stays as long as the weather allows it to.

Retailer normally welcomes paintings of their shops, walls, name boards. Since it makes the shop look cleaner and better. Their shops look alluring and stand out among other outlets. Besides rural households shopkeepers and Panchayats do not accept any payment, for their wall to be painted with product messages. To get one's wall painted with the product messages is seemed as a status symbol. The greatest advantage of the medium is the power of the picture completed with its local touch. The images used have a strong emotional association with the surrounding, a feat impossible for even a moving visual medium like television which must use general image to cater to greatest number of viewers.

A good wall painting must meet some criteria to generate awareness and remind consumer about the brand.

The most frequented shops can be painted from inside also one feet above the ground level.

It is courteous to take the verbal permission of owner. The permission is normally given.

However by taking the permission of the rural retailers or house owners, one gets the owner normally committed to taking care of wall painting.

A definite way of arresting is to use bright colours and these do not fade away easily. A good paint will survive the ravages of dust, sand and rainstorms for about three years.

It is found that ads which contain local content or which related to their culture are more noticeable.

The selling idea should be local to the target market to be more noticeable. Because the local selling idea is more easier to understand and hence catches the attention of the target consumer.

Villagers are more conservative buyers than their urban counter-parts. Their desire to innovate with new products is restrictive. As you know that most of the people in villages are farmers. But they have basic needs for consumers non-durable like soaps, shampoos, creams, toothpaste, tea etc., in consumer durable, they need clothes, TV, fridge etc., but due to lack of money they give more preference to price. They want cheap and quality product. So, they spend less on luxuries.

Another important aspect of advertising is media what kind of media should be used in rural parts of India. It is found that 90 per cent of rural people watch TV and 98 per cent of rural people see advertising and 60 per cent believes on ads shown or printed. But a large number of companies have used traditional media more effectively in rural parts of India to connivance the rural consumers. This is because through traditional media the message which is conveyed to the public in an entertaining way which related to their culture. So, it has more impact on the target rural consumers. But, TV is also a fast growing medium in villages. Hence, TV could also be an effective medium for the rural masses if the content of the ad message is entertaining, understandable and relating to their culture.

Another key factor in rural advertising is retailer in villages, the people's faith on retailers is very high. The people ask the retailer that "which product is better". So the companies should give more values to the retailers.

Another important aspect of rural advertising is at what time advertising should be peaked up in the rural parts of India? So, the answer would be the festive and post-harvest season. To derive maximum mileage their uses needs to be planned meticulously because during the post-harvest seasons, farmers have enough money to spend.

Finally, this market should be exploited by the advertisers because it is a big market and bulk of the Indian population resides in villages. Advertising professionals will have to tell them about the product through proper channel which is access to them. The better media mix leading by traditional media with TV, Radio, Newspapers, Magazines, Banners etc. The urban market is full with the products and services now companies will have to look for this rural market. Advertising professionals too will have to move to the rural India with new strategy.

7
Targeting the Consumer

Introduction

Marketing is all about targeting the consumer and reaching out to him/her through a variety of media.

The new trend among waring brands to indulge in campaign that targets its competitors and consumers with claims and counterclaims. The question is do such self-destructive campaign work and by indulging in a no-holds barred free for all fight, aren't brands lowering their commitment to consumers? Clearly. This is one marketing tactic that is guaranteed to be a sure fire candidate for the "worst practice" tag.

Not everybody however is taking their eyes off the consumer. A MART study on folk media analyses the different types of rural media that are currently available to marketers and how they can desire the campaign to meet different kinds of marketing objectives.

Serials and soaps on television channels are also vying for viewers attention. So a *Kusum* or *Kahani Ghar Ghar Ki* and a *Kyun Ki Saas Bhi Kabhi Bahu Thi* have to market themselves just as aggressively as the brands that sponsor these shows, to ensure that their TVRs don't nosedive. A CFAR monitoring study analyses some of the popular soaps on TV to identify trends in portrayal of their key characters, particularly women. After all, when the consumer and the viewer is the women of the house, they have to make sure that they are targeting her with soaps that appeal to her-never mind whether that so is branded *Kahani Ghar Ghar Ki* or Lux International.

An Eye for an Eye

Stray episodes of misleading claims/campaigns or signs of the things to come? Desperate situations call for desperate measures. That the consumer durable industry has been fighting in a sympathetic marketplace for a couple of years now is no secret. After giving discounts, offering freebies, wooing dealers and launching hi-decibel ad campaigns, the companies have been looking for new planks to protect their shares of a stagnating pie and sustain their razor–thin margins. Health appeared attractive enough to win over the coy customer. And thus followed the rush of tall claims.

Predictably, the rounds of tall claims are followed by series of allegations from competition that is fighting with its back towards the wall too. However, with all the country's mega brands making claims and counter-claims, where does all this leave the consumer? Confused? Sure. Distrustful? That too.

Gimmicks Galore

The claim was openly refuted by Rajeev Karwal, senior vice-president (consumer electronics), Philips India at the launch of the latter's Eye-fi series. The Eye-fi series, incidentally, is supposed to be fortified by an intelligent chip that adjusts the incoming transmission signal from the tower or the cable operator and gives a consistent picture to the viewer, reducing eye fatigue.

Commenting on the Golden Eye, which Karwal himself had launched during his earlier tenure in LG, he said: "The feature was developed as a unique selling proposition as LG had just entered the country and we needed to establish it in the customer's mind. Since wrinkle free fabric was coming into vogue and had become a buzzword, we started associating Golden Eye with it. It was positioned as a wrinkle-free technology and did not claim to take-care of the eyes as LG is doing now."

In their set of counter-claims, Mahalingam of LG says the intelligent chip that Philips is flaunting as part of its Eye-fi is merely a gimmick. Every hi-end television has a similar chip that irons out fluctuations in incoming transmission by about 2-5 per cent and adjusts the contrast, colour and brightness among a few given parameters, hardly enough to take away the eye-strain. Moreover, the chip costs merely a couple of dollars and is not a major technological breakthrough as is being projected, he says.

Talk to others in the industry and they say that both the features of Golden Eye and Eye-fi, are actually present in all hi-end TVs. The companies are merely trying to brand and position as breakthrough a routine feature, available with all in the industry. And the health angle? Most agree that sustained TV viewing is definitely bound to strain the eye, Golden Eye and Eye-fi not withstanding. Certainly, the consumer is not getting the true picture from either player.

Brand Equity at Stake

Further, LG produced tests conducted by IIT Delhi that declared capacity levels to be in accordance with the measured capacities with a maximum divergence of 2.9 per cent. Whirlpool lashed back saying the LG's cited measures were for gross volume instead of net volume and that IIT Delhi did not figure in the list of government approved testing labs. LG, of course, stood by its tests and considered itself vindicated of all charges.

What about the consumer? Confusion, understandably, reigns supreme. The educated consumer reacts to such information by developing a distrustful attitude towards every brand in the industry. Every such war of words greatly dilutes the equity of the brands involved. Certainly, not a good sign for an industry where most product categories are declining at worst and stagnating at best".

A Revolution in the Making

Organised retailing has for long been projected to be the sunrise industry. However, retailing in the New Millennium is a whole new ball game and Indian retailers, will have to be truly customer-savvy if they are to succeed in this business. The challenge for the retailer is increasingly how to convert footfalls into effective sales.

Retailing in itself has become a product and effective packaging is creating mega retail brands like Food World, Big Bazar, Shoppers Stop, etc.

This article is an attempt to understand how retail is packaging itself and targeting itself at increasingly demanding customers. Organised retailing has taken off in a big way in categories such as readymade garments, consumer durables, furniture, food, health care, entertainment and information systems. This article result of a study carried out on retail brands in the five major metros in the above-mentioned retail categories.

To establish its own identity in the consumer's mind, every retail store uses different techniques to create its own brand presence. There are some major common trends though which are being used extensively by the retail trade. We discuss the top 25 techniques, which retailers are using to target customers and build brand equity.

1. **Mall appeal.** The location of the retail outlet is perhaps the most important aspect of its positioning strategy. It's important that a retail outlet is located in one of the renowned plazas/malls unless of course it has a large enough property in a prime shopping area in the city. Delhi's Ansal Plaza, Mumbai's Shoppers Stop, Chennai's Spencer's Gurgaon's City Centre and Metropolitan Mall are some of the reputed shopping arenas in the country. These shopping malls offer the right kind of ambience and environment for sale of a large variety of items, right from clothing to cosmetics to gift items to health care products and more. But more importantly these

malls offer a shopping experience, which any stand-alone retail store is unable to offer. The experience is created due to a number of factors: the presence of open spaces, air-conditioned shops, swanky lifts, water fountains, wonderful lighting and most importantly food centres which in itself is one of the main attractions for potential shoppers.

The composite experience that these malls offer is the biggest component in the packaging of retail shops that are located within the malls.

2. **Making its presence felt.** How the store packages itself is the next most important point in an outlet's packaging dynamics.

   Merchandise display is very critical. The way the display is done depends on the space available, but the use of the space is also equally important. The bigger the space, bigger is the scope for the retailer to exhibit the merchandise effectively. The customer should feel awe-struck by the perfection of the display of the products.

3. **Special effects.** Often creating effects that are unique to the store can establish an identity for the brand. For instance, Kid's Kemp, India's largest retailer of toys, uses cartoon characters and clowns in colourful gear in its shop front to attract children. The dancing characters are a source of entertainment for kids and parents alike and helps create a shopping ambience that is fun, relaxed and unique. The experience within the store too matches the shop front experience thereby enhancing the identity of Kid's Kemp as a fun place for children and their parents.

4. **Store ambience.** Increasingly more and more retail outlets are focusing on improving in-store ambience. For instance, in food retailing, especially restaurants, the cutlery is also specially created with the name and emblem of the store etched on them. The walls are painted in a manner that goes with the overall theme of the store. Music inside the stores adds to the ambience. And in some outlets, children are given free gifts and an area where they can play. The furniture used inside such retail shops have become trendy, colourful, less space-consuming and innovative on design. In the retail outlets for general groceries, the carrycot besides providing convenience is also a major interest for kids. They even ride in them while their parent shops. The number of aisles that an outlet has, the placards, the lighting and even the design of the carpets make a statement about the ambience. For instance, the kids section in Kempfort has carpets with pictures of animals on them.

5. **Shopping assistance.** Friendly, smiling, young, energetic, well dressed, well versed retail assistants have added to the overall feel and look of the place. Communication with the customers has improved significantly and efficient shop assistants can actually enhance customers' satisfaction levels. In many shops, assistants often behave like a member of the customer's family, assisting not only with information about products but assisting in the care of toddlers while their mothers shop. The dress code, appearance of assistants, fluency in languages and knowledge of products add to the overall quality of a customer's shopping experience.

6. **All in the brandname.** The significance of the brandname is also very high in the retail revolution. The retail outlet has to communicate its USP quickly and significantly to its customer. Cafe Coffee Day, Barista, Music World, Food World, Shoppers Stop, Kidskemp are classic examples of retail brands that are now part of the Indian marketing lexicon. Crossroads, Big Bazar, lifestyle have also established themselves as brands to reckon with.

7. **Social bonding.** Many a retail outlet has gone beyond its brief of just selling products and services. The retail brand proposition is intelligently wrapped around a bunch of activities which go beyond the core competency. For example, the swanky. Shoppers Stop in Hyderabad routinely organises music shows and other entertainment gigs. The food chains offer customers the service of hosting their family celebrations–like a child's birthday party–on their premises. The retail outlets have innovatively positioned themselves wrapped around activities. The ability to organise such events elevates the outlet from just another retail outlet to a platform for social communication. Thereby, such outlets are easily able to integrate themselves into the lifestyles of their customers. And this association helps the outlet to establish a customer relationship that is focused not on customers' functional needs but on emotional needs).

8. **Facade.** The facade beckons a customer to step into a mall. The facade is the bait that gets a customer hooked. Kempfort in Bangalore does it with its fantasy inspired building that is reminiscent of a

majestic castle set in medieval Europe. Situated near the Bangalore airport, the building is one of the city's major landmarks. The large store and its amply stocked shelves are in sync with its communication of scale of operations. The Ansal Plaza in Delhi and Crossroads in Mumbai are more contemporary in structure, but they successfully communicate the theme of 'vastness'.

9. **Splashy hoardings.** The interesting outdoors hoardings attached to the walls of the plazas are essential elements in the packaging of the retail outlets. These not only provide opportunities for advertisements for the product, but also with innovation of technology and improvement in quality of hoardings, they attract attention to the plazas and malls. As the billboards keep on changing, they add a touch of newness from time to time to the facade of the plaza. Also if the billboards are well lit and innovative in proposition, they help to create much more sustainable impact in the minds of the consumer than the regular nameplate.

10. **Colour combinations.** Colour adds life to the product through its packaging, and similarly it adds life to the retail store. The colourful walls, shelves, placards, photographs on the open walls and colourful people around make these places beautiful. These also add to the attractiveness of the place and more people throng to the outlets.

11. **Projecting an image.** The retail outlets are trying to be more and more cerebral in their approach towards communicating their USP. And this is being tried in many ways–one of them is by projecting an image

that is in sync with the accessories in the outlet. The trendy image is being projected not just through the furniture but also accessories such as flower vases placed at selected points, live plants to add greenery at prominent comers of the shop, balloons and festive paper chains to highlight the roof, matching drapes and carpets that go with the theme of the shop. The concern for little details is aimed at uplifting the mood of customers and increasingly antiques and art pieces are making the walls of retail outlets more distinctive and helping in projecting a certain image, style and ambience. These little details also suggest to discerning customers that an effort is being made to touch the hearts and minds of consumers.

12. **Extras count.** Presence of other important centres, like a theatre, or a good parking place, a garden, a temple, a playground are some of the extra facilities that help to generate more footfalls in the retail store. It is increasingly becoming crucial for outlets to provide customers with more value for money, and more so in terms of experience, convenience and facilities. As the fight for the consumer's purse and hence her mind continues more and more retail stores are looking at every little thing that can provide them with the extra edge.

13. **Promotion.** Continuous promotion of the products that are being displayed on shelves is an important ingredient for attracting customers. The aim of every retail outlet is to attract genuine buyers and not just window shoppers. Continuous in store promotion goes a long way in this effort. The

customer finds it worth her while to visit the store again, if in the first attempt, she gets a freebie for the money that she has spent. The in-store promotion also offers customers with various discount coupons, either of the shop itself or of some other renowned outlets offering reliable branded products. There are also surprise gifts for children during birthdays, gifts on marriage anniversary for newly weds and a lot of prizes on contests that are a regular feature at such outlets.

14. **Winning with events.** A lot of retail outlets, specially those that deal in apparel, readymade garments, etc., organise local fashion shows from time to time. Such shows are beneficial for the outlet due to the fact that they are sponsored events and sponsors throw in a variety of interesting prizes to make it attractive for customers to be present on such occasions. For customers, it offers excitement, entertainment and a chance to win a prize or two. The fashion shows ultimately help in enhancing the image of the outlets and improve customers' experience with the retail brand. A win win situation for all concerned.

15. **Pathbreaking ideas.** Novel ideas that work for the product category as well as the retail outlet are not easy to come by. But pathbreaking ideas can help in building brand image and gaining customer loyalty. One such pathbreaking idea was introduced by Cafe Coffee Day which was the first coffee pub to offer net surfing facilities within its pubs to consumers who dropped by for a coffee. What worked for Cafe Coffee Day was that the facility

was introduced just when the Internet was taking off in a big way among youngsters and it immediately caught the attention of youngsters. Consequently, Cafe Coffee Day successfully associated the brand with being young, hip and cool.

16. **Right fit.** Packaging that is not in sync with the brandname, its USP and its image can backfire. What works for one brand is unlikely to work for another. It is for the brand to discover its ethos and to create an ambience, environment and accessories that suit its proposition. Me-too-ism can sound the death knell of a retail brand.

17. **Gateways to growth.** Hypermarkets are poised to be a big retailing-opportunity in India. Such retail outlets are big on the value for money proposition and the success of Big Bazaar is an indication that hypermarkets could well be the gateways to growth. Hypermarkets assure consumers of standard quality. But the big USP that they offer is the price point. Some hypermarkets have even claimed that if the consumer can prove that she has purchased any of the displayed items at a lower price point, that product would be given to her free.

18. **Courting consumers.** Food courts have become an essential part of the offering for a retail store as shopping and entertainment merge. Proximity of food vendors to the main retail store or location within the shopping mall is a key criteria. The footfall, if high in the mall, will also create pressure on the adjoining foodcourts and consumers would demand almost the same kind of standards that

they associate the shopping complex or the retail store with. The ability to offer a variety of cuisine with good sitting arrangements is clearly a major point in the packaging dynamics of the retail stores' marketing initiative.

19. **Surprise.** The ability to throw surprises at the customer is another ingredient in the packaging dynamics of a retail store. People do visit the same stores from time to time with the hope of getting surprises. This is true in many cases where the customer or his/her companion got the surprise for the first time. For instance, if a child visiting a store along with his parents gets a surprise gift on the occasion of his birthday, it is an occasion which he will remember for a long time. This pleasant association creates some kind of loyalty between the customer and the store. In anticipation of surprise gifts people keep going to a particular retailer when she could easily have gone to another one.

20. **Reinventing the mix.** It's mandatory for the retailer to discover a niche in the mind of the consumer and having created this positioning it needs to be recreated from time to time. The mall needs to be choosy in selecting the retailers so that the mix is harmonious and stores deliver continuous improved value to the consumer. Also for the retail store, it needs to get upgraded in terms of modernity of the merchandise, ambience of the interior and even the layout inside. It also needs to pick up some new brands, new promotions and offer a new zing. While renovation is essential, there is one word of caution:

by reinventing itself a retail outlet must take-care to see that it does not destroy the core values with which the brand is associated.

21. **Reward loyalty.** Customers who keep visiting the same store again and again love to be recognised. The need to be recognised is a human trait that can be exploited by retail outlets to their advantage. Privilege customer cards address this need by attributing points depending on the amount of purchases made. The points are redeemable through free gifts and cash discounts on future purchases and addressed by the fact that many outlets have privilege customer cards. Many have the system of attributing points depending on the amount of purchase. Honouring the loyal customer is the need of the hour-without the loyalty factor, the footfall starts declining.

22. **Buzz marketing.** The packaging of the retail outlet or the mall should be done in such a way that it creates a lasting impact on the minds of the customers. This gets translated in terms of positive word of mouth. This generates a buzz about a retail store or mall that is worth much more than the returns that advertising budgets and marketing spends can procure.

23. **Window dressing.** Creating window shoppers today is somewhat associated with creating potential customers tomorrow. Window shopping offers potential customers a chance of getting associated with the merchandise of the store without getting into the obligation of probable buying. The retail

outlet has to offer the facility of window-shopping, and it is directly associated with the physical packaging of the store. The layout and positioning of the showcases, the product and the kind of display arrangements are some of the most important parameters in this regard.

24. **Shopping facilities.** The consumer experience has to be smooth and hassle-free. Towards this end, it is imperative that retail outlets accept a variety of payment modes. Payments via credit cards and debit cards is increasingly on the rise and outlets that fail to accept these new payment modes stand to lose out on potential repeat customers. Acceptability of different modes of payment, say credit card, debit card apart from cash, is one element. Also the outlet has to assure its customers that the store will replace products that are found to be damaged/non-usable. The physical location of an ATM on the premises also helps in increasing sales.

25. **Touch and feel.** Physical proximity is required between the merchandise and the consumer. The consumer wants to touch and feel the product, study it more closely before making the purchase decision. The aspiration or urge to have the product becomes much stronger as the customer touches it and feels it. Merchandise that is displayed in a customer friendly manner has a high likelihood of being picked up by customers. Hence factors such as lighting, shelves at different heights, display of merchandise that offers easy access to customers are all critical aspects of retailing.

CAS: A Method to the Madness

CAS is a three-letter word that is causing much L angst in the living rooms of broadcasters and cable-operators alike. The system, spearheaded by the Cable Network Regulation Amendment Bill, aspires to get the consumer to watch only those channels she pays for. The system involves three distinct sets of participants. The broadcaster, the cable operator and the subscriber-consumer. The advertiser is being left out for the moment. There is some degree of tumult in every constituency. Lets go through some of the key issues at stake. There is plenty of muck around.

Let's start at the very beginning. At the start of it all, there was good old Doordarshan. Offering 'Satyam, Shivam and Sundaram' in its programming mix from day one. Capturing the imagination of a nascent mass of people exposed to television broadcasting for the first time round. The 1971 Indo-Pak war provided enough grist to get that part of the nation that could afford a black and white television set in their homes. And when there was no war, there was 'Krishi Darshan'! There was Bollywood as well! Remember Tabassum?

The days went by, the Asiad brought colour television broadcasting to the fore. Mrs. Gandhi (of the Indira variety) went gungho with the HPTs and LPTs all over the country, networking large tracts of the land with reasonably good quality broadcasting. To date, Doordarshan's reach remains wide and vast, challenging the best of distribution systems in the country. "Buniyaad" and "Hum Log" remain programmes that had TRP ratings that will never ever be repeated in the history of broadcasting in this land! The power of the singular channel was exploited to the hilt! All this came free. The cost of watching Doordarshan remained the acquisition cost of a television set and of course the cost of your local electricity supply! The choice of programming remained with the broadcaster who decided what the country must watch. The process: pretty much top down!

Then came cable. With it came excitement. The excitement of choice. One additional channel, and then another, and till a time when the channels multiplied like electronic rabbits. We have a choice of 92 in some cities today!

With cable came a service that had to be paid for. Want to watch more exciting stuff that had programming that depended on consumer insight, pay for it. A broad-spectrum payment plan that dissipated an average Rs. 150 over the bouquet of offerings your local 'cable-wallah' decided to offer you. Intermediation was the name of the game. It still is. The 'cable-wallah' will give you what he wants. He will charge you what he wants. He understands what the market can bear, and he will milk the price.

And now its time to bring some method into the madness of the flux around. Set-top boxes will have to be bought. The consumer can pay for the channels he watches. There is individual choice at the level of the consumer! The real numbers of cable households in the country will be revealed, in the medium term. Cable operators who hitherto suppressed numbers of subscribers will need to come clean. Do we really have 40 million actual C&S users? Or is the number as small as the ones that cable operators reveal (one fifth of it)? There is more exciting news. The real viewership base of each channel in question will be revealed soon. The advertiser, who primarily fuels the moneys in this business, will soon get to be savvier than he is today. Broadcasters will get more transparent in the touting of their channels.

The weaker ones will need to fall by the wayside and Darwinism of the media kind will prevail. The fittest will survive, seek out advertising revenues, and well get viewed by the largest chunk of choice-expressing and money paying consumers.

Folk Media Campaign Strategies

In 1919, Dipchand, a composer of swang used this popular drama form to motivate youngsters to join the defence forces.

In the 1940s, Indian Peoples Theatre Association, the cultural front for the Communist Party of India used folk forms like *jaatra, bhavqi, burrakatha* in the states of Bengal, Gujarat, and Andhra Pradesh to seek people's participation. Similarly other folk art forms like *alha* of Uttar Pradesh, *lavani* of Maharashtra, *gee gee* of Karnataka, *villupaattu* of Tamil Nadu and *kabigam* of Bengal were also used to generate public consciousness against British rule.

Post-independence, the government used folk media to promote awareness about the five year plans and other developmental activities.

Study Objectives

In a bid to understand how relevant folk media is today among rural consumers and therefore its relevance to media and marketing practitioners, New Delhi based

Marketing and Research Team (MART) conducted a study to explore the 'use of folk media for effective rural communication and advertising'. The study by Shivani Sohal and Pallavi Dua has tackled five elements of folk media: magic shows, puppet shows and interactive games Sohal and Dua's main objectives were to answer the questions that continuously crop up when marketing executives are exploring the available options for rural advertising:

- Is the present reach of mass media sufficiently deep into the rural markets?
- Is the medium accessible to rural consumers?
- Does the medium have the desired impact on the rural consumer's mind?
- Do rural audiences enjoy this form of communication?

TV Viewership

For television, they discovered that television continues to be out of bounds for a majority of the rural audience. Power is far from ubiquitous in our villages. In rural Gwalior alone, out of the six villages surveyed by the duo, five did not have power supply during the daytime. Second, community viewing is a common practice in the villages. This does not ensure either a regular audience or a fully attentive one. In Brijpalpur, a village with a population of around 2600, there were only 7 TV sets. Third reach and frequency of regional languages and vernacular programming being limited, it acts as a barrier to comprehension of messages. However, if the same communication was done in the local language or dialect, the comprehension factor would improve dramatically. Fourth, viewership is far from guaranteed. Even in TV owning households, women rarely get an opportunity to watch the programmes as they are busy with household chores during the day and do not watch in the presence of elders at night. Low involvement with the advertised messages is another barrier. The alien situations, context and ambience do not inspire confidence in the messages. A large number of people preferred the Escorts stall to the television commercial as the stall gives them a 'touch and feel' opportunity. Finally, rural masses experience a clash of values with television programming and hence rural audiences continue to resist the medium and its messages.

Radio's Losing Appeal

Radio has lost its popularity with rural audiences. Perhaps this is due to a combination of factors including the growing inroads being made by television as well as the declining quality in relevant programming choices for the rural masses. Consequently, across the study's sample of 88 respondents, only 10 said that they listened to the radio. According to the IRS 98, barely 20% of people in rural areas own a radio.

Other media, including cinema and print, have limited reach. While cinema is popular largely with young males, advertising through cinema is done only on a limited scale. Since the medium is not free, people have access to it only a few times in a year. Lastly, due to social taboos, this medium is practically inaccessible to women and young girls. The low level of literacy is the single most important factor in the lower reach of print media. Besides, accessibility of mainline publications is limited due to erratic availability.

Evaluating Folk Media

The researchers evaluated some of the campaigns that used folk media and analysed their impact on the following parameters:

- Reach
- Interaction
- Credibility
- Persuasiveness
- Product suitability
- Costs.

Here we excerpt some of the main findings of the study on the efficacy of folk media on the above parameters.

Nautanki

- *Reach*—The project involved social marketing of contraceptives. The decision to use folk media was triggered by the observed trend of decreasing efficacy of video van campaigns. Nautanki enjoys immense popularity in the villages because of its narrative style and rustic humour. Its audience includes people of all ages. The kids are the first to be on the spot and grab the best seats available. Word of mouth is the best form of publicity for such events. The attendance of women, however, is comparatively low. Some of them who want to watch the shows do so in groups from their rooftops. This is partly because the shows are held at night when women are not allowed to come out of the houses. The other reason is that nautanki has a negative association in the social context and it is considered inappropriate for women from respectable homes to be seen at such shows.

- *Interaction*—The element of interaction with the audience is among the most interesting aspects of such a medium. The performer elicits feedback from the audience to involve them and also to gauge their level of interest and retain their attention. Sometimes dummy performers are present in the audience and at the appropriate moment he is included in the play. For instance, the Eveready campaign uses this strategy very effectively. One of the artistes approaches the venue in the dark carrying a torch. The ray of light pierces the darkness and distracts one of the performers on the stage who asks: "Who is there? What is it that shines so brightly".
- *Credibility*—The show is usually set in a village ambience and since the performers are familiar with the rural set up it lends a lot of credibility to the message. Sometimes the audience trusts the performers to the extent that they are willing to take their advice on the product being advertised. For instance, in the case of Hindustan Latex's nautanki, several villagers approached the performers for details about the family planning methods that had been talked about the usage of contraceptives, availability, safety and price. For the show, some women performers had been deliberately selected so that women in the audience could discuss the issues freely with them after the show.

- ***Product suitability***—The nautanki scripts can accommodate all types of products-from contraceptives to tractors, fertilisers to tea. This medium gives an opportunity for discussion of sensitive issues. And since the performers talk about these issues on stage, they help to break inhibitions regarding the product or the issue.

- *Persuasiveness*—The scripts are designed to explore every issue of concern regarding the product. All aspects are discussed from availability to product advantages and price-so that there are no questions unanswered and nudges the potential consumer towards a purchase decision. In the case of the Swasth Gram Pariyojana, the script explains the benefits of having a small family; discusses the different brands of contraceptives available; removes misconceptions regarding usage and side effects; and finally directs the target customer towards the Swasth Gram Pariyojana clinic or the anganwadi worker with whom it is available.

- *Costs*—Nautanki involves a large team of 7-8 members and hence the cost of the campaign rises. The costs include food and lodging, travelling, infrastructure, safety of female performers and other contingencies.

- *Success Factors*—Scripts have to be flexible so that on the spot improvisations can be made to suit the local dialect, tastes and preferences. The performers should be sensitised to make the changes by gauging audience response to the issues being discussed. For instance one of the artistes in the Hindustan Latex project altered the script in some villages where he felt that the audience was not quite comfortable when the family planning techniques were being talked about. At the same time, some issues were deliberately raised so as to make people uncomfortable and thereby force them to think about what was being discussed.

Magic Shows

- *Reach*—This medium is highly entertaining and has a great appeal to audiences. Though sometimes perceived to be a 'kid's medium' by advertisers, as well as audiences, this folk form draws a mixed audience.

- *Interaction*—The magician calls children, involves them in the tricks and adds humour which greatly enhances the attentiveness of the audience. For instance, during the RC&M mela, the magician had "turned" one of the children into a hand pump and had water flowing out of his ears continuously. This amused and amazed the kids in the audience tremendously.

- *Credibility*—The credibility is considerably lower for such a medium because of its illusionary nature and this has a rub-off on the messages as well. The audience may enjoy the show but it may not result in any decisive action.

- *Product suitability*—Products targeted at children are best suited for this medium because of its perceived association with them. Also, the medium seems to work best for almost all product categories where the attributes of the product can be woven into the magician's trick. For instance, the Britannia Tiger biscuits and TVS' Max 100 campaigns both used the same ribbon flowing trick. While in the Britannia show, the magician remarks "after eating Tiger biscuits, the heart beats as fast as this ribbon," in the TVS show, a similar declaration is made: "TVS Max 100 can touch high speeds as easily as this."

- *Persuasiveness*—Because of the low credibility levels, persuasiveness is not very high. It is very good for increasing product awareness, explaining certain attributes but its effectiveness in converting all this into action is questionable.
- *Costs*—It is a relatively inexpensive medium when compared to folk theatre. The number of artistes is limited to one or two at the most. Preparation time is much less and since the tricks performed are more or less the same, changes are made only in terms of adapting the trick to the message.
- *Success Factors*—Entertainment is the key to magic shows. And hence product categories that lend themselves to this folk art form are best suited for such shows. Serious issues cannot be raised through this medium.

Men, Women and the Family

Ever since private satellite channels started beaming into our homes, soaps have dominated prime time television. Their supremacy has been challenged only once–and that too for a short phase–by the phenomenally successful gameshow, *Kaun Banega Crorepati (KBC)*. But soaps are back in fashion again. The New Delhi-based Centre for Advocacy and Research (CFAR) undertook a monitoring study to understand trends in gender representation on television. CFAR monitored three satellite channels–Zee, Star Plus and Sony and three terrestrial channels–Nepal TV, Ekushey TV and BTV to get a feel of South Asian programming trends. Best practices presents excerpts from their findings.

The quantitative study looked at 50 hours and 30 minutes (101 episodes) of fiction during the early months of 2002. In all 52 episodes, from satellite TV channels and 49 episodes from terrestrial channels were monitored.

Setting of the Serials

The setting/locales in the fiction on satellite channels is entirely urban. Only on NTV (Nepal TV), 24% of the settings have a rural ambience. NTV also has a significant presence of foreign locales while on the other channels, it is entirely absent.

Milieu of the Serials

The study shows that on the urban landscape, "less privileged homes" do not feature at all on Zee, Sony, Star as the favoured setting. The lives, conflicts, joys and aspiration of the upper and affluent classes form the backdrop for the family saga on TV. Terrestrial channels (5%) appear to give some representation to "less privileged homes".

Activities Performed on Screen

Interaction at home is the favourite activity across channels Star (84%), Sony (56%) and Zee (53%). Among the total interactions at home, women are involved in upto 57% of such exchanges. But significantly for the men, this category is equally high at 43%. Interestingly, the most popular activity is talking on the telephone, be it a mobile or a landline. This is especially true of Sony (15%) and Zee (11%). The telephone is more popular among those in the 22-30 age group (13%) and among the retired people (8%).

Occupation

Homemakers (26%) top the list in keeping with the belief that TV serials target mainly adult stay at home women. Self-employed persons in business (25%) are the next popular category. These people belong primarily "to the upper and" affluent classes. Students (20%) form the third significant category. Both satellite and terrestrial TV channels register more female than male students.

Age of Characters

Satellite TV focuses primarily on the 22-30 age group, far more than terrestrial (satellite, 52%, terrestrial, 34%). Terrestrial channels appear to be more representative in their depiction of different age groups. There is also a significant presence of the older generation in satellite channels.

Marital Status

Interestingly, the representation of married characters (55%) is higher than that of unmarried characters (38%) on satellite channels. In contrast, terrestrial channels have a higher representation of unmarried persons (58%) than married ones (38%). Gender-based representation is interesting, insofar as divorced or separated men feature more than women and among the widowed, women feature more than men. This is explained by the presence of grandmothers in most serials.

Appearance

The appearance of men on TV is predominantly modern (80%) as compared to women who appear more traditional in dressing and get up (64%). Traditional symbols like the *bindi, mangalsutra* and *sindoor* are visible across all channels. Homemakers are largely portrayed as traditional while professional and self-employed men and women are modem in their appearance.

Qualitative Findings

The aim of the study has been to examine the representation of gender in TV fiction. The quantitative and qualitative analyses indicate that gender representation must be seen in the context of the depiction of the family.

The TV Family

The family in TV fiction is found to be cross-roads: it is striving to maintain its traditional status in the post-modem era where the only certainty is that everything is in a state of flux. The notion of family is continually changing, adapting to the reality of increasing urbanisation and even globalisation. The TV family is profiled through an analysis of a selection of 15 episodes of the sample. It is found that faith has been renewed in the traditional values of the Indian family system in a number of ways: from the way characters dress to the central issues being addressed by the serials. However, it is also apparent that the traditional family has been portrayed in modern terms perhaps in order to appeal to the urban audience which forms the main target audience of satellite TV fiction. The packaging of TV fiction thus becomes a very important aspect of its analysis. In the packaging process we discover that the family is constantly under threat, that conflicts within the family and their resolution lie at the centre of the narratives, that the narratives follow a dialectic process through which tradition undergoes a kind of present day *agnipariksha* and comes out with its fingers burnt but more resilient, albeit changed.

Relationships

Sexuality often presents the greatest challenge of all. The way male and female sexuality is depicted in these serials is extremely revealing about the sexual mores within society. The man-woman relationship also demonstrates "the packaging" concept: adultery is as commonplace in Hindi serials as it is in foreign ones. It is conducted openly and, sometimes flaunted. This frankness about extra-marital affairs may be interpreted as a sign of modernity. However, TV producers are very deliberate in such depictions. First, the extra-marital affair ends in failure. Usually, the dutiful wife plays the moral card and triumphs over the confused and errant man. Secondly, the affair is lent legitimacy because the man is often "forced" into a marriage against his wishes, and so his extra-marital affair with a woman he loves is acceptable, even natural. The fact that his wife is not allowed the same license is part of the typecasting so frequent in these serials.

Joint Families Dominate

The TV family is almost invariably a joint family, primarily Hindu. Over two-thirds of the monitoring sample dealt with the traditional extended family as opposed to the modern nuclear family. In this sample, had two Muslim dramas - Heena and Sarhadein. Significantly, even here the family structure goes beyond religious differences: the Hindu and Muslim families in these serials are very similar. For instance, Sameer's family in *Heena* (Sony) is like Abhay's in *Kusum* (Sony). To this extent, there is a certain uniformity in the character of the family.

Gender

This joint family is predominantly a male construct. In a few instances, the daughters of these families continue to live with their parents even after marriage. The usual circumstance is that of marital discord or divorce and less of widowhood.

Nuclear Families

Within this overwhelming presence of the joint family, a small space has been carved out for the nuclear family. In serials such as *Justujoo, Saanjjhi, Kalash, Mehendi Tere Naam Ki,* the household consists of one independent family or just one married couple. The profile of the family from an economic perspective, shows a basic correlation with members of the joint family being usually rich, and work in the family business (95%) while nuclear families in serials tend to be middle class. There are variations: in *Kohi Apna Sa, Justujoo* and *Mehendi Tere Naam Ki* the main characters are professionals.

RESUTLTS & ANALYSIS OF QUESTIONNAIRE

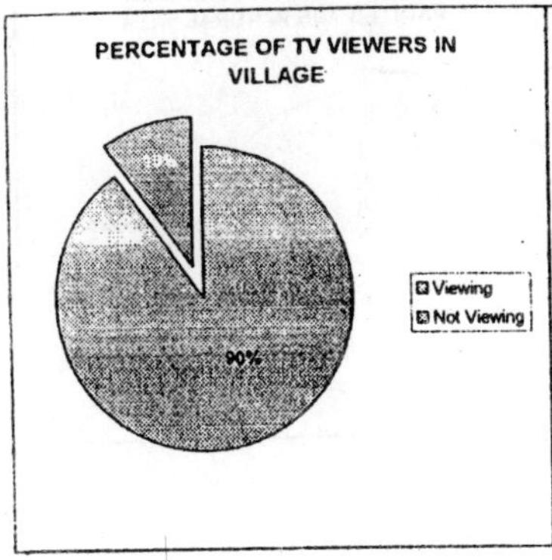

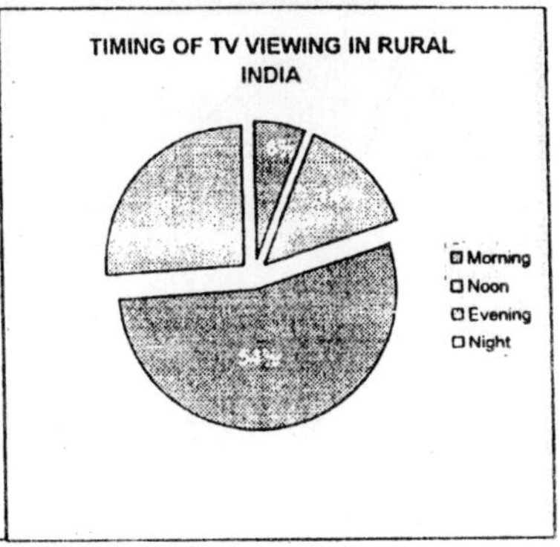

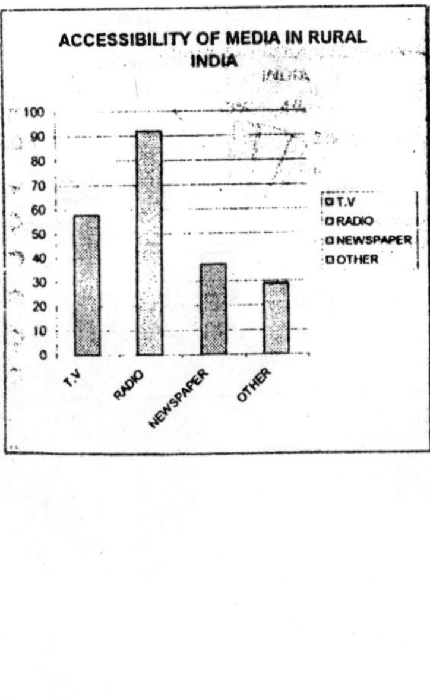

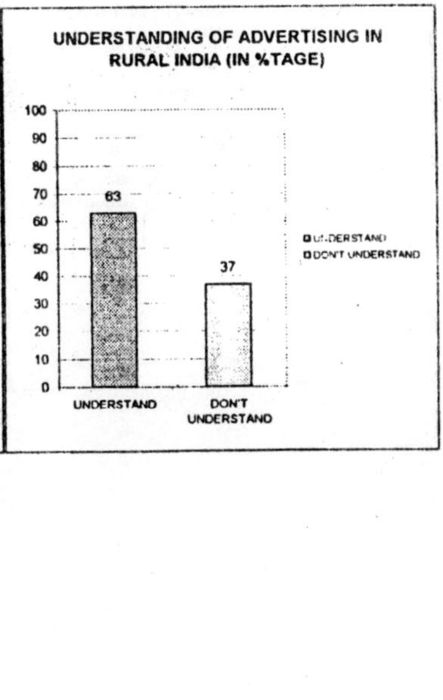

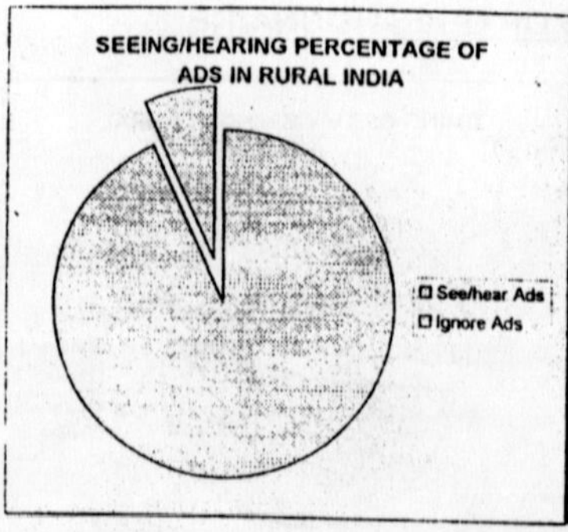
SEEING/HEARING PERCENTAGE OF ADS IN RURAL INDIA
See/hear Ads
Ignore Ads

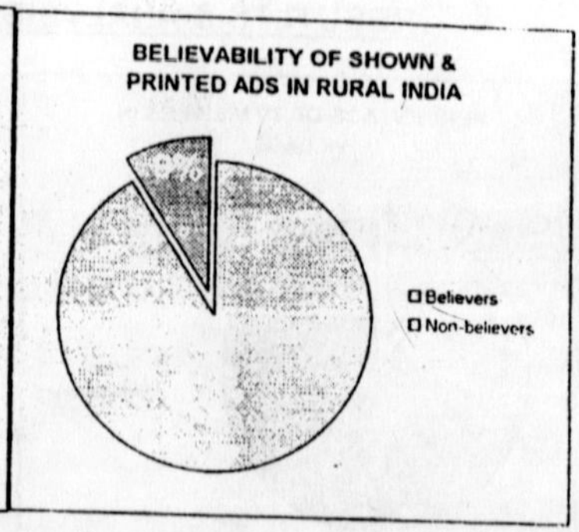
BELIEVABILITY OF SHOWN & PRINTED ADS IN RURAL INDIA
Believers
Non-believers

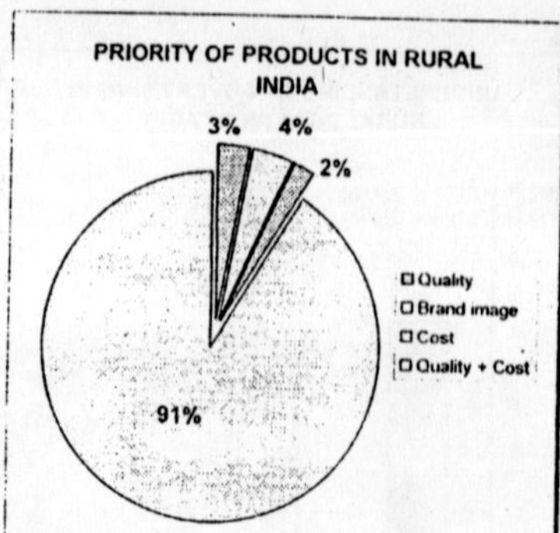
PRIORITY OF PRODUCTS IN RURAL INDIA
3%
4%
2%
91%
Quality
Brand image
Cost
Quality + Cost

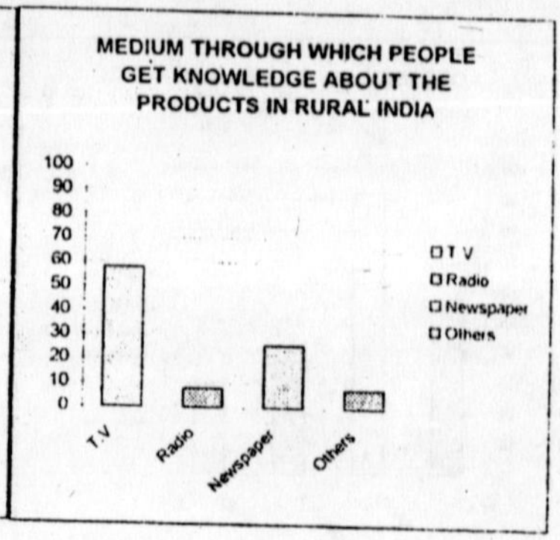
MEDIUM THROUGH WHICH PEOPLE GET KNOWLEDGE ABOUT THE PRODUCTS IN RURAL INDIA
100
90
80
70
60
50
40
30
20
10
0
T.V
Radio
Newspaper
Others
T V
Radio
Newspaper
Others

PERCENTAGE OF PEOPLE BUYING PRODUCTS WHICH IS AGAINST THEIR CULTURAL VALUES IN RURAL INDIA
2%
98%
BUY
NOT BUY

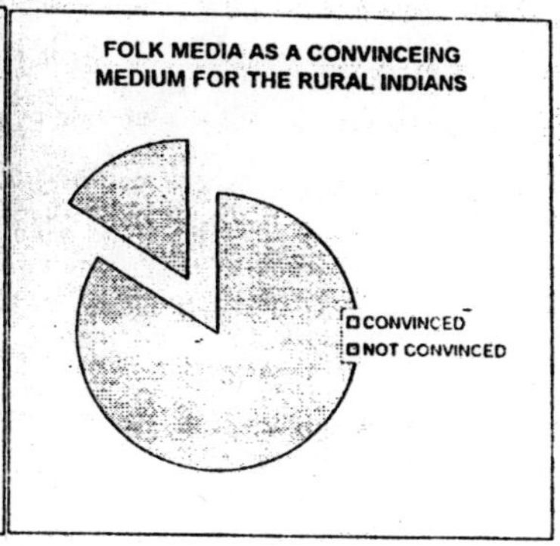
FOLK MEDIA AS A CONVINCEING MEDIUM FOR THE RURAL INDIANS
CONVINCED
NOT CONVINCED

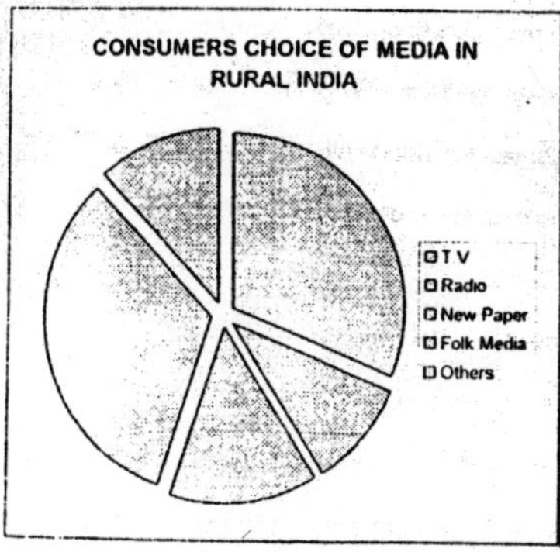
CONSUMERS CHOICE OF MEDIA IN RURAL INDIA
T V
Radio
New Paper
Folk Media
Others

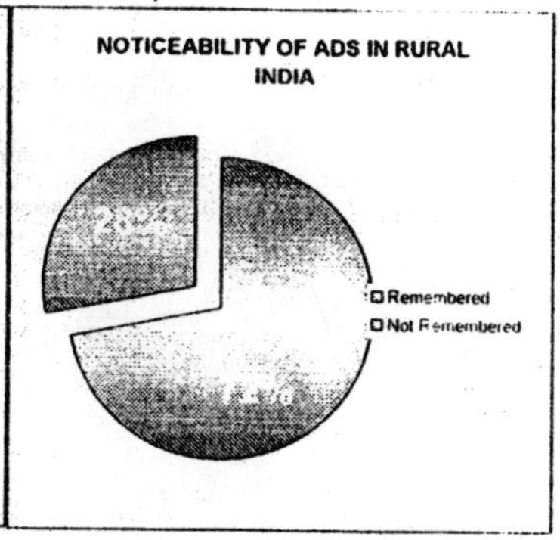
NOTICEABILITY OF ADS IN RURAL INDIA
28%
Remembered
Not Remembered

8

Importance of Business Communication

"Communication is the art of transmitting information, ideas emotions and attitudes from one person to another".

Communication is essential in any group of human being. It is required everywhere. Communication is essential in family, hurch, group, class of students, organization etc., communication transfers through from one person to another. Communication is the task of imparting information.

Every business organization function through planning, organization, staffing, direction and controlling. In fact these are the mains and basic functions of business management. Without communication management cannot perform its duties smoothly. Modern business is very complex. Its nature has been changing very rapidly. Communication plays pivotal role in modern business. According to Harold Janes, Communication in business world has always been a world of actions. Preparation of samples, undertaking production, making exchange of human efforts, formulating policies, imparting training all these activities require effective Communication. At the advert of liberalisation, Privatisation and Globalisation, whole nature inevitable for taking advantage of technologies development. We can explain the importance of effective communication in the following words:

1. **Size of Business:** The size of business understandings is increasing due to many reasons. Business enterprise has to open branch offices at different places in order to have a proper co-ordination between branch and head office, the concerned officer has to keep liaison through different types of communication methods.

2. **Specialisation:** This is the age if specialization. Everybody wants to become expert in his spheres. Specialisation always invites departmentalization. Each department should be in touch with the happenings in other departments. For instance, production department has to collect information from sales debarment and stores department. Unless there is a close interaction between the department. Things will not move in the proper direction.

3. **Tremendous Competition:** In the present situation, competition in business has reached to the cut throat level. The skillful salesmanship can help to increase the sales of business

4. **Organisation:** Effective communication is must for efficient salesman. Attractive advertisements are used to improve the sales line of the organization.

5. **Harmony:** Every manager in the modern business tries to maintain harmonious relations with his staff. It is very essential to minimize the chances of strikes, lockouts etc., which may affect the interest of both.

6. **Motivation:** The continuous dialogue would definitely improve the layout management relations. Training, meeting and discussing always boost the moral of the workers. Due to effective dialogue, manager comes to know the hidden ability of his subordinates, which can be used fully for the development of the organization.
7. **Image Building:** Each business organization has its own personality. Image of the organization, to the greater extents, is dependent on the desire of the organization regarding public relations aspect.
8. **Policy Formulation and implementation:** Indians are good planners but bad executers. Proper and meaningful communication can bridge the gap between planning and implementation. Many times, good plans don't see the light of a day because of non-cooperation on the part of executive. This should not happen.

"Communication is an exchange of facts, ideas, opinions, emotions, by two or more persons".

Above two definitions clearly indicate that communication is a process. It is continuous process. It is always two ways. Communication requires message. Unless, you have some things to say or express, communication doesn't take place. Information, ideas and emotions are transmitted through communication process. Message may be transmitted through words, picture, graphs, voice, gestures, actions etc. The communicate must understand transmitted message. He should respond in a given time. The process of communication can be shown as below.

Management is an art of getting the workdone. In order to get the workdone by specific person, communication is essential in the initial stage ideas are formed and they are encoded. Encoded ideas take the shape of message, which is sent to communicate by using proper media. After receiving the message, a communicate interprets and analyses it. It is called decoding of message. The quality and effectiveness of decoding is dependent on the transmitted by communicate to original communicator, the process of communication becomes complete.

Therefore, process of communication involves the following steps:

1. The ideas are formatted in the mind of communicator.
2. The communicator encodes formed ideas.
3. Encoded ideas take the shape if message.

The message is transmitted through proper media to communicate.

Message is received, interpreted and analysed by the communicate.

The communicate sends the reply to the communicator. It is called feedback. Here communication process of cycle completes.

The message is transmitted through proper media to communicate.

Message is received, interpreted and analysed by the communicate.

The communicate sends the reply to the communicator. It is called feedback. Here communication process of cycle completes.

Nature Scope and Importance of Business Communication

Business communication is related with the study of communication between individuals and groups engaged in the process of administration and management of an organization. Therefore it is always goal oriented.

Communication is interchange of thoughts, opinions of information. One way communication informs the receivers whereas two-way communication is exchange of information an ideas. Today there is no such thing as one-way communication, in fact, it is always two-way process involving transmission and reaction. Feedback is core part of every business communication because it is necessarily an action oriented affair. A two-way communication established and builds lasting relationships between people.

Business communication takes place within the set up of an organization. Therefore, it is governed by certain norms and conventions. The members of an organization communicate as insiders.

Business communication is characterized by a serial reproduction of messages. Messages are sent from one person to another, and person to still another, and so on to other persons of an organization. It remains interpersonal.

Importance

In every business a large amount of communication is oral and written. According to research any organization. Functions through planning, organizing, staffing, directing and controlling. In fact, these are the main and basic functions of business management. Without communication, management is not possible. Modern business is very complex. At the advent of liberalization, privatization and globalisation whole nature of business is changing rapidly. Mergers are taking place. Mass use of computer has become very essential. We know that managers dose everything through communication.

Business enterprises have to open the branches at various places. In order to have a proper cop-ordination between branches and head office, the concerned officer has to keep liaison through different type of communication methods.

Principal of Effective Communication

Communication is a process of transmitting the ideas. It is a two way process. Transmitted message should be completely understood by the person who is at destination. As far as possible message should be kept brief. The knowledge level of the Communicate has to be taken into consideration. Able communicator dissent waste his time in unwarranted communication. Need and objective of the communication should be analysed in advance. Normally, the executive, who is responsible for the communication, keeps following principals in mind.

Clarity If Objective: The communicator should be known to the communicator. Why communication is necessary? He should be completely able to answer the question.

Proper Messenger: The communicator should construct the message in meaningful manner encoding of thoughts in an intellectual task and it has to be done with proper care and thinking.

Knowledge of Communicatee: The Comunicatee should understand the message sent by the communicator. He should be competent enough to analyze and to respond. It is only possible when communicator knows minute details of the communicate. Effective Communication is dependent on level of knowledge of Communicate and his status in the organization.

Selection of Media/Method: In order to have effectiveness in terms of cost and benefit, proper selection of methods is essential. Again it depends upon the nature e.g., communication and urgency.

Removal of Barriers: Some time misinterpret ion of message may cause confusion in the organization. All possible hurdles are removed. Curtailment of message in the barrier of Communication. All such factors should be taken into account.

Feedback: There should be inbuilt capacity in the communication to motivate the communicate to respond. Respond/reply is a core part of communication. Communicatee is expected to react to themes sage. Feedback helps to complete the communication cycle.

Barriers to Effective Communication

Communication is a two way process. It is not a one-way business with lack of feedback. Successful performance of an organization depends on effective communication. The key to success is found in the manager's ability to communicate effectively. Barriers are the hurdles of difficulties that come in the way of Effective Communication. They are physical, Psychotically, linguistic, cultural and mechanical in nature. In business organization the major barriers arise because of its set up. Therefore, these barriers are termed as organization barriers. Generally the physical distance between employees of an organization and the specialization of activities are the main organization barriers. Authority and status relationship also create obstacles in the communication process.

Barriers to Communication may be broadly classified as below:

Physical Barriers

(i) *Complete stimulus:* It becomes very difficult to pass on the message orally, if another conversation given information simultaneously within hearing distance, sometimes loud music or traffic noise creates barrier in the communication process.

(ii) *Environmental Stress:* A strong glare puts hindrance in case if visual communication. Because of undesired strain on the eyes of communicatee, message is not received properly. A high temperature, humidity, bad ventilation etc. contribute in distortions in the sending and receiving of message.

(iii) *Subjective Stress:* Due to sleeping, ill health, consumption of drugs, mental strain etc. communicator cannot interpret the message in desired manner.

(iv) *Ignorance of Media:* User should be well conversant with media that is adopted for conveying the message. The use of a media with which the receiver is not familiar would turn the media itself into a barrier. For example, the use of visual media like maps and charts to instruct workers, who have not been familiar with the maps and charts would switch off their attention for lack of knowledge of the media.

Psychological Barrier

Every person has his own ways to look at the world, at people at events and situations. A way of thinking of a person many times takes a shape of strong base of communication. No two persons possess accurately similar frames of reference.

Following are some psychotically barriers:

(a) Unjust Assumptions: The unjust assumptions are a common barrier to communication. It creates a lot of misunderstanding. A manager, for example, incorrectly assumes that the subordinates understand the technical terms he adapts to give instructions.

(b) Barrier of Illness: Illness is the attitude of people with closed minds. They think that they know everything about a subject. Usually they are not prepared to accept that they could be mistaken. Many make the generalised statements. Examples of such statements are given here.

1. Globalisation is dangerous to India.
2. Women cannot become superior to men.
3. Insincerity s thae base of business.

An attitude of illness is an outcome of biased approach.

(c) Snap Reactions: Snap reaction are a resinous barrier in communication process. Some listeners tend to pass remarks criticize the communicator even through his communication is not completed.

(d) Apathetic Listener: The apathetic receiver is psychologically dead to your communication. He is indirferent to 'speaker.

(e) Sophisticated role: The reviver is not willing to learn from the communicator. That means he is unreachable. In such situation, the communicator should try to create right impact. He should change the communicator's perceptions from 'I already know that to Ah! that's a different angle'.

(f) Defensibleness: Man always tries to justify himself. He thinks that admitting is take means a loss of face. Therefore he tends to rationalize the mistake that he commits. This type of attitude of the communicatee is a great hindrance in the effective communication journey.

(g) Fear: Fear is clearly destructive to communication. Therefore, the ordinary objective must be to eliminate fear. A fear give rise to slow and narrow thinking the candidate's misinterprets the questions asked by the interviewer. In the answer paper, the wrong answers are written by the nervous students.

Phonetic Barriers

1. **Linguistic and cultural barriers:** In Business communication language is the central element, a language is the expression of the thoughts and experiences of a people in term of there cultural

conditions. The language used indifferent culture takes different colours and meaning. It comes under the influence of the accent of the local language.

2. **Mechanical barriers:** In-group communication whistling microphone and incorrect placement of loudspeakers are disturbances. Mechanical barriers include any disturbances, which interferes with the fidelity of the physical transmission of the message. A telephone is poor working order creates mechanical barrier. In mass communication, mechanical barriers also include smeared ink in the printed matter, a rolling screen on television, a type too small to be read in the newspaper etc. Good business communication is a two way process. It requires the communicator to try and ensure that the message is received properly by the communication. Therefore, mechanical devices used for the communication need frequent checking and proper maintenance.

Written Communication

Written communication is a non-direct communication. Main job of any office is to communicate through written words. Letters are write, record is kept, notices are issued, memos are prepared, billings is done. These all activities are written communication. The shortcoming of oral communication have paved the way for mass use of writing communication.

Written communication is the most effective means of communication. In any situating. It is one-way process. The ABC of written communications accuracy, brevity and clearly. Written communication is necessary and most effective where the need of information is permanent, the topic requires detailed explanation accuracy and precisions in wording is essential and the audience is large and widespread.

The following are some written communication usually used in the business organization.

- Business letters
- Memos
- Reports
- Notices
- Proposals (Advertising Brief, Purchase, New Products etc.)
- Agents and Material etc.
- Printed material (Advertising Material like Broachers, Folders, Leaflets, Giveaways, Point of Purchase Material etc.)
- House journals (newsletters)
- Agreements documents
- Directives and instructions

Advantage of Writing Communication

1. Written communication can be kept as legal records which may be used in court matter.
2. Written communication can be used as future reference.
3. They are formulated more carefully than oral communication.

4. Secrecy .cannot be maintained in written communication.
5. The success of written communication largely expends on ability to interpret the communication by the receiver.
6. Language may be barrier of writing communication.
7. The written communication is not useful where illiterate people are working in India, It is a great problem.

Business Letters

A business letter is permanent record for the business. It can be used for further correspondence.

It is possible to increase the business by sending business letters to the various parties it helps to promote the sale of the organization.

Business letters act as a representative of the organization and it creates goodwill in the market.

It is very useful in collection the due from the customer.

The complaints and misunderstandings of the customers can be removed by the way of giving them satisfactory replies.

The status enquiries can be made through the letters, which is essential for taking the decision in respect of sending the goods to new customer.

Business letter can be used as a legal evidence in the court.

Memos

Memos both printed and memorandums (commonly called memos). Memorandums of course, are letters written inside the organization, through some companies use them in outside communication. Memorandums are primarily the written messages exchanged by employees in the daily conduct of their work.

Variation in Form

Memorandum are often short some companies use 5 x8.5 inch stationery for them as well as the conventional 8.5 x 11 inch size. Memorandums are usually initiated by the writer rather than signed.

Large organizations, especially those with a number of location and departments, often include, additional information on their memorandum stationary. Department, Plants, Locations, Territory, Store Number and Copes to are examples. Since in some companies memorandums are often addressed to more than one reader, the heading to may be followed by enough space to list a number of names.

Report

The British Association and Industrial Education has defined a report as a document in which a given problem is examined for the purpose of conveying information as a report, finding, putting forward ideas and sometimes, making re-communications.

A report is an account or statement which describes an opinions, situation etc. Which is the outcome of observation. A report is prepared after the thorough enquiry. In a report a specific problem is discussed at length. Therefore, reporting mans relating what has been learning by observation, enquiry or investigation and writing on account of it.

Types of Report

1. Factual report
2. Oral and Written reports
3. Formal and informal reports
4. Routine and Special reports
5. Personal and Impersonal reports

Importance of Report

The reports play a very important role in the business organization. They provide information for the purpose of planning and control. It is natural that the larger the business organization the greater the need for planning.

1. Decision making—Decision making is one of the important function of management sound decision making is dependent on the reliable information.

2. Performance evaluation—In order to evaluate the performance of various, the reports are demanded.

3. Vehicle of communication—A good communication system brings the prosperity to the business organization. Proper dialogue between the workers and management reduces the chances of conflicts.

Report Purpose

The reports are prepared for the following purposes:

(a) To enable the preparation of various budget.

(b) To determine the requirement of personnel.

(c) To improve the quality of production.

(d) To get information regarding the market.

(e) To know the causes of labour unrest, decline in sale and other business problems.

House Journals

Printing of House Journal responsibility generally lies with human Resource Development Department of every organization. The purpose of printing House journal is for the private circulation within the organization. Circulation is within each departments of the organization for the purpose of informing each individual the developments going around in the organization e.g. if you are appointed in a company, then HR department informs each and every individual in the organization the you are appointed as a Manager in Marketing Department. Sometimes your achievements like achieving the marketing targets is also informed to everyone, which motivates others to perform like yourself. The purpose of House Journal is nothing but achieving C 2 P 2 – Customer, Community, Profits and Public goals of the organization.

By printing House Journal Public relations are maintained within the organization.

Print Material (Advertising Material like Brochures, Folders, Leaflets, Giveaways, Point of Purchases Material, Labels, Stickers, Direct Mailers, Catalogues, and Prospectus etc.

"Advertising is a salesmanship in print" – this means advertisement should talk like a successful salesman. What is a salesman? The person who is presentable, friendly, knowledgeable, technically qualified, having pleasing manners, good-looking etc., if your ad can talk like him it is going to do a great job.

Importance of Body Language

Regarding the importance of body language, management consultant Nancy Austin says, When people don't know whether to believe what they are hearing of what they are seeing they go with the body language-it tells the truth. You can play fast and loose with words, but its more difficult to do that with gestures. Psychologist Paul Ekman says, 'we talk with our vocal cords, but we communicate with our facial expressions, our tome of voice, our whole body.'

When you can consciously 'read' what others are saying unconsciously, you can deal with issues at work and it home–before they become problems. In every special and society, those which are in control try to appear large, strong and fearless.

The classic example is the soldier standing at attention in the presence of a superior officer. His body is extremely tense and in perfect symmetry-signs on subservience. It is their status and role relationship that is reflected in this way.

Facial Expression

A popular saying goes like this 'the gace is the index of the heart.' Whatever we feel deep within ourselves is at once reflected in the face. It is very important in any face-to-face communication event. We convey such a lot without a word. For example, let us consider the facial expressions generally associated with happiness, surprise, fear, anger, sadness bewilderment, astonishment and contentment. Let us also consider a smile, different kind of smiles, of frown, corners of lips, the position of the eye brows, cheeks–whether drawn up or back or dropping, the jaws, nose/nostrils and the chin. We can easily mark all by looking at ourselves in mirror. The thoughts and feelings conveyed may be positive or negative. It follows, then that we can change our behaviour/expressions by changing the inner nature. But it is not easy. Much depends on how deeply we are and what constructive efforts we make to stay calm and relaxed, and send out positive signals to make the best of every given situation. Every facial muscle is an instrument of communication.

Eye Contact

Everyone knows that eye contact is of paramount importance in all face-to-face communication when we look at somebody's face we focus primarily on his eyes try to understand what he means. The eye, along with the eyebrows, eyelids and the size of pupils convey our innermost feelings. Eyebrows and eyelids raised and combined with dilated pupils tell us that the person is existed, supervised or frightened.

If the eye contact is brief, or we take our eyes off the person very soon, it indicates nervousness or embarrassment on our part. Of course, eye contact and eye movement convey their meaning in combination with other facial expressions.

Gestures

In addition to facial expressions and eye contact parts or move in a very in a meaningful manner. These movements are called gestures i.e. the physical movement of arms, legs, hands, terse and head. They play a very important role in conveying meaning without using words. For example, pounding first on a table shows anger, a forefinger held high above the head shows 'numberi' and a forefinger and a thumb touching to form a circle stands for 'ok'. In the same way, arms spread apart convey the meaning of 'wide', shuffling form one leg to another means 'nervous' and a terse and extended, slightly forward, has been interpreted as 'intense'.

It has been observed that intensity of a speech directly associated with the size of a gesture. The great the gesture, the louder the speech. Speech and gesture go to together, and therefore have to be properly coordinated. In the absence of speech-gesture-co-ordination we experience confusion and discomfort.

Appearance

Appearance, for our purpose, includes clothing, hair, jewellery, cosmetics etc. All these may seem unrelated to body language. But on having a closer look we find that they are very meaningfully related to our face, eyes, gestures, posture etc.

Famous writer has said that a man is recognized by his 'dress and address'. Dress does not need any explanation. By address he means the say a person speaks to other. Every occasion has its own particular type of dress. It may be formal or informal. It is normally, a part of an organization's work rules to have a formal suit or combination of jackets and trousers for the working hours. Certain organization have a uniform for all levels of workers. If one changes from the formal dress to informal or casual he is easily noticed, and his dress speaks volume about his attitude to life, to work, to his colleagues and his own feelings. That is also the reason why invitation cards to formal occasions like cocktails, receptions, dinners just the dresser clothes that are important for any occasion but also shoes, hair style, perfume etc. that convey 'meaning' in non-verbal form.

Advantage of Body Language

(a) Body language is the most easily visible aspect of communication. It, therefore, helps the receiver of the message in decoding the message.

(b) Body language complements verbal communication. Specially in face-to-face communication, no message can be completely sent across without the accompaniment of facial expressions and gesture. It helps in establishing report.

(c) Body language adds intensity to the process of communication. In the absence of any gesture, change of posture, proper eye contact any face-to-face communication will look bland or inspide.

(d) Because people care for body language it goes a long way to improve the overall atmosphere and looks of the organization. A resourceful message can make effective use of it.

Limitations of Body Language

(a) Since it is non-verbal communication, relying or gracing expressions, gestures etc., it cannot be wholly relied on. Words written or spoken can be taken seriously, but body language cannot always be taken seriously.

(b) People belonging to different cultural background send out different signals. They are therefore, liable to be misinterpreted. One has, therefore, to be very careful in there use and understanding.

(c) Facing expressings, gestures, postures etc. become infective in face-to-face situations, that means there are just two or a small number of participations in the communication situation.

Meeting Management

From time to time, the staff participates in business meetings. They will range from extreme formal to informal. On the formal end will be conferences and committee meetings. On the informal end will be discussions with groups of fellow workers. Weather formal or informal. The meetings will involve communication. In fact, the quality of the communication will determine their success.

Participants role in a meeting will be that of either leader or participant. Of course, the leader's role is the primary one, but good participation is also vital. The following paragraphs review the techniques of performing well in either role.

Techniques of Conducting Meetings

How you conduct meeting depends on the formality of the occasion: Meeting of such groups as formal committees, boards of directors, and professionals organizations usually follow generally accepted rules of conduct called parliamentary procedure. These vary specific rule are too detailed for review here. When you are involved in a formal meeting, you would do well to study one of the many books covering many parliamentary procedure. Before the meeting. In addition, you should know and practice the following techniques. For less formal meetings, you can depart somewhat from parliamentary procedure and those techniques. For less formal meetings, keep in mind that every meeting has goals and that such departures should never hinder you from reaching them.

Plan the Meeting

A key to conduct a successful meeting is to plan it thoroughly. That is you develop an agenda (a list of topics to be covered) by selecting the items that need to be covered to achieve the goals of the meeting. Then arrange these items in the most logical order. Items that explain or lead to other items should come before the items that they explain or led to. After preparing the agenda, if the meeting is formal, make it available to those who will attend. For informal meetings, you may find keeping the agenda in mind satisfactory.

Follow the Plan

You should follow the plan for the meeting items by item. In most meetings the discussion tends to stray and new items tend to come up. As leader, you should keep the discussion on track. If new items come up during the meeting, you can take them up at the end or perhaps postpone them for a future meeting.

Move the Discussion Along

As leaders you should control the agenda. When one item has been covered, bring up the next item. When the discussion moves of subject, move it back on subject. In genial, do what is needed to proceed through the items efficiently. But you should not cut-off discussions before all the important points have been made.

Thus, you will have to use your good judgment. Your goal is to permit complete discussion on the one hand and to avoid repletion, excessive details, and useless comments on the other.

Control those Who Talk Too Much

Keeping certain people from talking too much is likely to be one of your harder tasks. A few people usually tend to dominate the discussion. Your task as leader is to control them. Of course, you want the meeting to be democratic, so you will need to let these people talk as long as they are contributing to the goals of the meeting. However, when they begin to stray duplicate, or being in useless matter, you should step in. You can do this tactfully and with all the decorum of business etiquette by asking for other viewpoints or by summarizing the discussion and moving on to the next topic.

Encourage Participation from that Who Talk Too Little

Just as some people talk too much, some talk too little. In business groups, those who say little are often in position lower than those of other group members. Your job as leader is to encourage these people to participate by asking them for their viewpoints and by showing respect for the comments they make, even through the comments may be illogical.

Control Time

When your meeting time is limited, you need to determine in advance how much time will be needed to cover each item. Then, at the appropriate times, you should end discussions of the items. You may find it helpful to announce the time goals at the beginning of the meeting and to remain the group's members of the time status during the meeting.

Summaries at Appropriate Places

After a key item has been discussed, you should summarize what the group has covered and concluded. If groups decision is needed the groups vote will be the conclusion. In any event you should formally conclude each point and then move to the next one. At the end of the meeting, you can summarize the progress made. You should also summarize whenever, whatever a review will help the group members understand their accomplishments. For some formal meetings, minutes kept by the secretary provide this summary.

Techniques for Participation in a Meeting

From the preceding discussions of the techniques that a leader should use, you know something about the things that a participant should do. The following review emphasizes them for you.

Agenda

The purpose of an agenda is to inform participants of the subject of the meeting in advance and to structure the discussion at the meeting itself. To inform people beforehand, and to solicit ideas, you should circulate a draft agenda and ask for notice of any other business.

Still before the meeting, you should then send the revised agenda with enough time for people to prepare their contributions. If you know then make this explicitly clear so that there is no confusion.

The agenda state the purpose of each section of the meeting. There will be an outcome from each section. If that outcome is so complex to assimilate by the participants. The understand of that summary for all other interested parties to see. This form of display that summary for all other interested parties to see. This form of display will emphasize to all that meeting are about achieving defined goals–this will help you to continue running efficient meetings in the future.

Follow the Agenda

When an agenda exist, you should follow it. Specifically you should not bring up items not on the agenda or common on such items of other bring them up. When, there is no agenda, you should stay within the general limits of the goal for the meeting.

Participate

The purpose of meetings is to get the input of everybody concerned. Thus, you should participate. Your participation, however, should be meaningful. You should take only when you have something to contribute and you should take whenever you have something to contribute. Practice your professional etiquette skills as you work courteously and cooperatively with others in the group.

Do Not Talk Too Much

As you participate in the meeting, be aware that other people are attending. You should speak up when you have something to say but do not get carried away. As in all matters of etiquette, always respect the rights of theirs. As you speak, ask yourself whatever what you are saying really contribute to the discussion.

Cooperate

A meeting by its very nature requires cooperation from all the participants. So keep this in mind as you participate. Respect the elder and he or his efforts to make progress. Respect the other participants, and work with them in every practical way.

Be Courteous

Perhaps being courteous is a part of being cooperative. In any event, you should be courteous to the other group members. Specifically, you should respect their rights and opinions, and you should permit them to speak.

Your Most Important Tools are

Clarificationa—Always clarifies: the purpose of the meeting, the time allowed, the rules to be observed (if agreed) by everyone.

Summary—At each stage of the proceedings, you should summarize the current position; and

Progress—This is what we have achieved/agreed; this is, what we have reached.

Focus on stated goals—At each divergence of pause; refocus the proceedings on the original goals.

Code of conduct—In any meeting, it is possible to begin the proceedings by establishing a code of conduct often by merely stating it and asking for any objections (which will only be accepted if a demonstrably better system is proposed). Thus if the group contains opinionated windbags you might all agree at the onset that all contributions should be limited to two minutes (which focuses the mind admirably). You can then impose this with the full backing of the whole group.

Writing for Meetings

Taking minutes—Usually it is the group's secretary who takes the minute–that is, takes notes during the meeting of what is said and decided. If there is no secretary, the chairman must assign the task to one of the participants, preferably a volunteer.

If the role of secretary falls to you, remember that it is better to have too many notes than too few. Jot down all the important points, decisions, and arguments, and who made them. Use language you feel comfortable with.

Minutes—Minutes of meeting are kept for several reasons.

They provide proof that members of a group came together, discussed certain issues, and reached certain decisions. Without such a record, any or all of this could be forgotten, or in the event of a large dispute denied.

They provide a useful reference for anyone unable to attend the meeting. A quick glace will enable him or her to grasp what its highlights were and what decisions were taken.

They help to hold participants to their promises, and to turn their promises into actions–the minutes record all such commitments and oblige the participants to report the outcome back to the group.

Writing up the minutes–write up the minutes as soon as possible after a meeting, while events are still fresh in your mind..

Before you start, check on the custody style. Look at copies of past minutes and consult the organization's standing orders.

Remember the two vital rules of keeping minutes–be clear and be objective. Don't use technical language or abbreviations that could puzzle any likely reader: the aim of minutes is to clarify, not obscure, the business and outcome of a meeting.

Distribution—Once you have typed up your official version of the minutes, show it to the chairman for his approval, and then run-off a number of copies. Circulate these to all members who attended the meeting to members who should have been there but where not, and to any other people you think should know what happened and was decided.

Communication Networks

With this degree of complexity there is some system for structuring who will communicate with whom. These systems are communication networks regular patterns of person-to-person relationship through which information flows in an organization. Two kinds of networks exist: formal and informal. Formal Communication Networks are systems designed by management to dictate are so simple those they may hardly be noticeable; in a large organization, they communication networks are with organization.

Downward Communication

Downward Communication occurs whenever superior intimate messages to their subordinate.

- **Job instructions**: Directions about what to do or how to do it. When you restock the shelves, put the new merchandise behind the old stock.
- **Job rationale**: Explanations of how one task relates to other tasks. "We rotate the stock like that so that the customer won't wind up with state merchandise."
- **Procedures and practice information about rules, regulations, polices and benefits.** 'Don't try to argue with unhappy customer. If you can't handle them yourself, call the manager.'
- **Feedback information about how effectively a person is performing.** "You're be really catching in fat. If you keep up the good work you will really catching on fast if you keep up good work you will be assistant manager by the end of the year".
- **Indoctrination:** Information aimed at motivating employees by impressing the organization's mission upon them and specifying how they should relate to it. "People can buy the stuff we sell at other place, but we can bring them in here by giving them what they want quickly and pleasantly. If we do that we will all come out ahead."

Most managers would agree at least in principle. That downward communication is important. It is hard to argue with the need for giving instructions, explaining rationale, describing procedure, and so on. Like their bosses, employees recognize the importance of downward communication.

Upward Communication

Messages flowing from subordinates to superiors are labeled upward communication. Many leading business attribute there success to the emphasis on upward communication in their organization. Upward communication can convey four type of messages.

- "What subordinates are doing we'll have that job done by closing time today".
- **Unsolved Work Problems**: We're still having trouble with the air-conducers in the accounting office.
- **Suggestions for Improvement**: I think I've figured a way to give people the vacation schedules they want and still keep out staffing up.
- **Task coordination**: Let's get together this afternoon and set up a production schedule.
- **Problem Solving**: "It takes three days fir my department to get report from yours. How can we speed things up?"
- **Sharing Information**: "I just found out that big convention is coming in town next week so you ought to get ready for list of business."
- **Conflict Resolution**: "I've heard that you were complaining about my work to the boss. If you not happy. I wish you'd tell me first."

- **Building Rapport**: "I appreciate the way you got that rush job done on time. I'd like to say thanks by buying lunch when its convenient."

Informal Communication Networks

Confirming: Some informal communication confirms formal messages. You have probably heard this sort to an experienced confirmation, yourself. The boss is really serious about cutting down on long distance calls time. I heard him yelling about it when I walked past his office.

How subordinates feel about each other and the job. I'm having a hard time working with Louie. He seems to think I'm mad at him. "Or I'm getting frustrated. I've been in the same job for over a year now and I'm itching for more responsibilities."

These messages can benefit both subordinates and superiors and this example why one survey showed that organization members find upward communication to be the most important and satisfying kind of on the job interaction.

Horizontal Communication

A third of organizational interaction is Horizontal Communication (something called lateral communication). It consist of messages between members of an organization with ezual power. The most obvious type of horizontal communication goes between members of the same division of an organization: office workers in the same department, co-worker on a construction project, and so on. In other cases, lateral communication occurs between people from different areas: accounting calls maintenance to get a machine repaired, hospital admissions calls intensive care to reserve a bed, and so on. Horizontal communication serves five purposes:

Expanding. Information communication can fill in the gaps left by incomplete formal messages. You might say to an experienced co-worker. "The invitation to the office party says casual dress." What does that means-jeans and T-shirt or sport coat and tie?

Expediting. Informal networks can often deliver messages more quickly that official channels can. Canny job hunters, for example, often use personal contacts to learn about openings within an organization long before the vacancies are published.

Contradicting. Sometimes informal networks contradict official messages. You might learn from a friend in accounting that the deadline for purchases on this year's budget isn't as firm as it sounded in the comptroller's recent memo.

Circumventing. Informal contacts can sometimes help you bypass official channels that are unnecessarily cumbersome and time-consuming. Your tennis partner who works in duplicating might sneak in an occasional rush. Job for you instead of putting it at the end of the line.

Supplementing. Sometimes even management realizes that informal communication can get the job done beter than the more formal variety can paradoxical as it seems, many companies elevate informal communication to an official policy by encouraging open, instructed contacts between people from various parts of organization.

Type of Communication

Face-to-Face Communication

Face-to-face communication comes may forms. Some are one to one meeting, either scheduled or spur of the moment. Other involves small groups of people, gathering spontaneously or in informed meeting. Still other face-to-face communication occurs in large groups, where one more speakers make presentations to an audience. Whatever the setting and number of people, all types of face-to-face communication is its speed. Once you make contacts with your audience, there is no time lag between the transmission of a message and its reception.

A second advantage of face-to-face communication is the control it gives you as the speaker. You might spend hours drafting a memo, letter, or report only have the recipient scan it superficially or not read it at all. In a personal contact, however, you have much more command over the receiver's attention. The listener at least has to pretend to pay attention and if you use the speaking skills described in the following chapters, your message ought to be clear and interesting enough to capture

Another enormous advantage of face-to-face communication is that is permits instantaneous feedback. When you speak directly to one or more listeners, your listeners seems confused, and you can speed up if details aren't necessary. Your can revise hurriedly if you have used the wrong word and offend or confused your audience. Because of the tremendous amount of feedback available in face-to-face communication, it has been termed the 'richest' kind of communication channel.

Teleconferencing

Face-to-face meeting may be desirable often makes them impractical. Teleconferencing is billed by its promoters as the next best thing to meeting in person. Video-conferencing allows participation in two or more locations to see and speak with each other. Until recently, most video-conferencing requires elaborate studios at each location, which made the technology unaffordable of all but the largest organizations. New 'desktop' conferencing using personal computers is putting the medium in reach of more workers.

Document or Computer Conferencing

This is another form of teleconferencing. This technology replaces face-to-face individuals to work on documents that are 'shared' via computers. As one person makes suggestions or changes a document the other can view that change on their own screen. Document conferences can take place in real time, with participants interacting via their independently but picking upon the comments and input of others in their ground. Communication experts have developed computer software (called group decisions support system of ('groupware') that facilitates electronic conferencing.

Telephone and Voice Mail

Telephone can be a useful tool group communication as well as one to one contacts. Audio-conferencing allows a group geographically separated people to speak via telephones.

Real time communication isn't the only type of telephone communication. Voice mail is the 1990s version of the answering machine; many communicators have voice mail, often with justification. Some voice mail menus and sub-menus can take forever (if you want information about schedules) and clever greetings can be annoying. But voice, just as you spoke it without the omissions and distortions that come when an intermediary transcribes your message. Sophisticated voice-mail system 'date-stamp' a message, letting the other person know precisely when you called.

Written Communication

Written communication comes in a variety forms. Letters, memos, bulletin, and other reports are familiar fixtures in almost everybody's carrier. Written message have a different set of advantages and drawbacks than their spoken counterparts have. Unlike speech written future reference–either to your delight or to your undying embarrassment and chagrin. While people may have trouble accurately recalling what you said a few hours ago, they can refer to your written remarks year later. Even if the receiver has lost or foregotten your message, you can always supply a copy from your files.

Along with its permanence written communication can be easier to understand that speech. Readers can study complex passage as many times as necessary a luxury they do not have when the same message is delivered orally.

Principal of Good Listening

Following are the principals of good listening.

1. **Psychological Process.** Listening is the concept which includes psychological factors. Physiological efforts.

Are required to understanding and retain the verbal materials presented in spoken form.

2. **Attention.** Listening is a turning or to another. It is a turning into the wavelength of the person trying to communicate. It is much more than a mechanical switching on or off.

3. **Active Process.** Listening is an active process. Listening means alertness and interest visible in the posture and expressions. It is also seen in the questions raised and comments made by the listener.

4. **Understanding.** Listening is not only making sense out of sound but also understanding what the speaker is saying. This is not as easy as sounds, because words have many meanings and people understand the same words differently.

5. **Fact and Fancy.** Listening means being able to distinguish between fact and fancy it view or our own attitudes and distorted interpretations of the speakers words cannot termed as good listening. There should not be selective listening.

6. **Tiring Process.** Listening is an active, physically and mentally tiring process. Listening efficiency is at its highest during the first 10-15 minutes and lowest during the last 10 minutes, during which stage the listening is mechanical.

7. **Lack of Selective Listening.** Paying attention only to what re-enforces our point of view or our attitudes and distorted interpretation of the speakers words cannot termed as god listening. There should not be selective listening.

8. **Sensitive to Physical Signs.** Listing involves the skills to mark out the signals. The listeners should be sensitive to all physical signs. The nervous habits and the gestures communicate the message which is non- verbal.

9. **Presence of Barriers.** There are common barriers to listening, it includes prior ability, distracting, burden, prejudice, snap reactions, premature evaluation etc.

10. **Training and Guidance.** Listening efficiency can be improved by about 255 through proper training and guidance, listing is a human skill deliberately cultivated. The expert goes a long way in efficiency.

11. **Fast Process.** Listening is a fast process. The rate at which we listen than the rate at which we speak. The listeners find time during which they analyze and evaluate the arguments.

12. **Complexity.** Listening is a difficult function. It involves many psychological and physical barriers. It is not easy to bring total perfection in the listening especially in the meetings and conferences.

8. Sensitive to Physical barriers. Listening involves th[illegible] skills to check out the agenda. The listener should be sensitive to all physical [illegible]. The [illegible] and [illegible] to [illegible] communicate the message [illegible] which is [illegible] verbal.

9. Presence of Barriers. There are [illegible] to listening [illegible] prior [illegible] [illegible] in [illegible] evaluation.

10. [illegible] and [illegible] [illegible] [illegible] through [illegible] and [illegible] [illegible] skill deliberately cultivated. [illegible]

11. Fast [illegible] [illegible] [illegible] which we [illegible] [illegible] the rate at which we speak. The listeners [illegible] time [illegible] [illegible] analyse and evaluate the arguments.

12. [illegible]

Index

A

Above the live media, 29
(The) Advertising Agencies Association of India (AAAI), 26
Ads aimed at
- men, 82, 84
- women, 80-81, 84

Advertising, 29
- nature, objective, 47
- purpose, 55
- parties using, 55-56

Advertising agencies
- principal functions (19th century), 16
- role, 66

Advertising Media Types, 57
Ad space buying, 16
Advertiser
- benefit of advertising to, 22

Advertising campaign, 66
Ambience of store (impact of), 159
America 18th century advertising, 12
American marketing system 19th century, 14
American Marketing Associations definition of advertising, 19
Appeals used in advertising, 64
Appearance (impact of), 205
Aquafina Ad, 114
Attention getting headlines, 64
Audio conferencing, 220
Axe Deodarants Ad, 115

B

Bad taste in Advertising, 49
- study, findings, conclusions, 51-52

Bathroom fittings ad, 118
Beauty products ads, 119
Beer ads, 82
Below the live media, 29
Benefits/harms of advertising, 38
Bisleri ads, 114
Body language, 203-07
- advantages, 206
- limitations, 207

Books on advertising, 30

Brandname
- significance of, 160

Brand Equity (techniques used to build), 157
Britain advertising 18th century, 12
Broadcast Media, 30
Budgets of advertising, 48
Business Communication
- nature, scope, importance, 191

Business letters, 199
Buzz marketing, 166

C

Cable TV in India start, 169
Cafe Coffee Day—idea of surfing, 163
Cartoons and Clowns, 158
CAS (Set top boxes), 168
CFAR (Centre for Advocacy and Research), 178
- study on trends on TV serials, 178-80

Changes in advertising, 17
Children advertising to, 45
Cinema, 172
Classified Advertising, 128
Classes of Advertising, 125
Clothing Ads, 123
Codes used on TV, 95
Coke's Rural initiative, 138
Cold wars, 48
Colgate Ad withdrawn, 49, 52
Colour combinations, 161
Communication
- meaning, 18
- importance, 187
- process-steps, 190
- types, 219
- networks, 214
  - types, 215

Communication Analysis of Ads
- Maaza, Milkman, Diet Coke, 113
- Bisleri, Aquafina, 115

Comparison of products, 66
Computer conferencing, 220
Consumer
- Advertising, 24
- benefits of advertising, 22

Cooperative Advertising types, 129
Copywriters (early times), 16
Cosmopolitan Magazine, 136
Creating ads, 66
Creative advertising, 68
- for different media types, 68

D

Definition of advertising, 12, 17-20
Demonstration, 148
- types, steps in, 148

Denim ad, 120
Dialogues on TV, 94
Diet Coke ad, 113
Direct Advertising, 29
Direct Contact, 148
Direct Mail, 59
Document (computer conferencing), 220
Dominance of males (announcement in ads), 107, 111

Dotcoms ads, 121
Double entendre in ads, 84
Downward Communication, 215

E

Economic effects (advertising), 69
Effective Communication
- importance, 188
- principle of, 192
- barriers to, 193

Effects of advertising, 69
Eisenhower's Presidential Campaign, 71
Electrical spectaculars, 61
Emami shaving cream ad, 119
Emotional appeal, 64
Ethics of advertising, 33
Ethical Principles, 36
Evamode Inner Wear, 135
Events organising (impact of), 163
Extra facilities in centres—impact of, 162
Eye contact—impact of, 204
Eye-fi series (TV) claim, 155

F

Facade, 160
Face to face communication, 219
Facial expression, 203
Factual approach, 64
Fair and Lovely ad, 49, 52
Family notion on TV (trends), 180
Female buying attitude—overlooking by media, 108
Female nudity and success of advertisement, 105
Female role portrayal as sex objects
- and buying attitudes, 106

Films and sex, 76
Financial Advertising, 127
Folk forms, 170
Folk Media Campaign
- evaluation, 173
- strategies, 170
- MART study, 171

Folk Theatre/songs—Forms in India, 146-47
Food courts—impact of, 164

G

Gender in advertising, 102
Geographical spread as basis, 23
Gestures, 205
Ghoshal (HTA) on Indian advertising, 27
Global Advertising, 24
Global Audience sensitivity, 46
Golden Eye Claim (LG), 155
Good advertising, 27
Good listening principles, 221
Gross Billing of advertiisng in India at present, 26

H

Haats and Melaa, 149

Health Drinks
- promoting, 112

History of advertising, 9
HLL's new rural initiative, 139
Hoardings, 161
Horizontal Communication, 217
- Purpose, 218

House Journals, 202
Hugo Perfumes ad, 117
Hypermarket
– USP of, 164

I

IBS (Indian Broadcasting Society), 26
ICC (International Charmbers of Commerce), 40
- Guidelines on advertising on Internet (1998), 39
  – scope, 42
  – definition, 42
  – basic principles, 42
  – disclosure of identity, 42
  – Costs and Responsibility, 43
  – respect for public groups, 44
  – users' rights, 44
  – advertising to children, 45

Indian Advertising in, 26
Indian Newspapers Society, (INS), 26
Indian Society of Advertising (ISA), 26
Indian Women—role/status, 101
Industrial Advertising, 25, 130
Indian Sexuality mindsets, truth, 73
- changes in, 77

Infant Foods Act, 49
Informative Advertising, 126
Informal Communication Networks, 217
Innuendo in ads, 84
Institutional Advertising, 127
Internet, 30 guidelines to advertising in, 39

J

Jadore Perfume Ad, 135
JK Tyre Rural Marketing Programme, 139
Joint Family in TV, 182

K

Kamaśutra ad, 49, 52

L

Language used on TV, 94
LG Products Golden Eye claims, 56
Linguistic and cultural barriers, 196-97
Liquor ads, 111, 132
L'Oreal Ad, 134
Lovable Cotton Essentials Ad, 134
Local Advertising, 24
Loyalty
- rewarding, 160
- of consumers, 15

Loyola Institute of Business Administration Chennai (LIBA), 139

M

Maaza ad, 112
Magazines, 58
- sexual advertising in, 99-100
- advertisement portrayal of women, 101

Magic Shows evaluation, 176-77
Mailing lists, 59
Mall Appeal
  – technique, 157
Man's Sex Appeal, 79-80
Manufacturer advertising, 15
Market Research, 67
Mass communication
  – means of, 21
Mechanical Barriers, 197
Media selection, 68
Media used in advertising, 28
  – types, 29, 57
Meetings, 207
- agenda, 210
- conducting, 208, 211
- planning, 208
- techniques, 207, 210
- writing, 213

Memos, 200
- variations, 200

Merchandise Display, 158
Milkman Ad, 113
Mineral Water Ads, 114
Minutes of meeting, 214
Misleading claims of ads, 154
Modern advertising, 13
Moral Principles, 37
Motivation Research, 68

N

Nature of advertising, 34
National advertising, 24
Nautanki evaluation, 173-76
Negative advertising, 48
New Technology of Broadcasting and Advertising
  – changes, 17
Newspapers, 29, 57
Nivea Ad, 135
Non-personal communication (advertising as), 18
Novelties, 62
Nuclear Family Serials (TV), 182
Nudity and erotic content, 88
- acknowledgement, 108

O

Objections/criticisms to advertising, 34-35
Objectives of advertising, 47
Obsession Perfumes Ad, 117
Organized Retailing, 156-57
Other Media, 30
Outdoor media, 30
Outdoor signs, 30
Oyzterbay Jewellery Ad, 134

P

Packaging (suitable), 164
Painted bulletins, 61
Perfume/deodrant ads, 82, 87, 115
Persuasive advertising, 125
Philips rural marketing programme, 139
Phonetic Barriers, 196
Physical Barriers to communication, 194
Physical attractiveness
 —criteria, 88
Point of sale-displays, 62
Political
- advertising, 71
  —criticism, 71
- effect of advertising, 71

Pornography—Indian scene, 76
Postcards (advertisement space in), 142
Posters, 61
Pressman Advertising and Marketing, 28
Print Media, 29
Print Material (types), 202
Process of advertising, 17
Production of ads, 69
Product characters, 65
Professional advertising, 25
Projecting an image, 161
Promotion of Products, 162
Promotional offer, 48
Psychological barriers to communication, 198
Puppetry use in advertising, 144
Puppet Theatre in India, 145

R

Radio, 59
- in advertising, 17
- Loss of appeal, 172

Reading/understanding TV, 96
Red Tape Ad, 122
Reebok Shoes ad, 122
Regulatory Bodies for Ads (India), 50
Reinventing the mix, 165
Relationships on TV, 181
Repetition, 66
Report, 200
- type, importance, 201
- purpose, 202

Representative Codes (TV), 94
Research in advertising, 16, 67
Retailing, 156-57
Retail Advertising, 129
Retailers in village, 151
Retail outlet-packaging, 166
R.K. Swamy BBDO health care (and social and marketing division), 142
Romantic appeal, 81, 109
Romance (use) in selling to a woman, 109
Rural Advertising aspects, 151
Rural Market for Advertising, 137
Rural Marketing Course, 139
Rural Spending, 138

S

Selling to a woman, 81, 109

Serials and Soaps on TV—Ratings, 154
Set Top, Boxes, 169
- implications, 169-70
Sex Appeal in Advertising, 77-78
- effectiveness, 86
- criteria of man, 78
- used to appeal to women, 80
- male/female views, 84-85
- spread, 86
- effective group, 84
- impact on society, 89
- discouraging moves by consumers, 89-90
- regulations, 90
Sexual imagery in ads, 87-88, 100, 105
Sexual theme, 64
Sexual arousal vs attractiveness, 84
Sex in
- Media, 90
- TV, 97
- TV ads, 98
Sexual advertising, 98-99
- in magazines, 99
- products using, 100
Sexuality (Indian)
- concept, mindsets, 73
Sexual stereotypes
- of women, 104
- and cultural expectations, 108
- male/female, 111-12
Shoes ad, 122
Shopping Assistance, 159
Shopping facilities, 167
Shopping Malls, 157
Signs, 93, 95
Sitcoms—sex in, 98
Slogans, 65
Soaps (daily), 177
- viewership, 177-78
Social bonding, 160
Social codes in TV, 93
Social effects, 70
Special effects in advertising, 158
Specialised advertising, 28
Speciality Media, 30
Splashy hoardings, 161
Sunsilk Procolor Ad, 119

T

TAG Heuer Watch, 136
Target group as basis, 24
Targeting customers—techniques of, 157
Technical codes used in TV, 93
Techniques of advertising, 62, 64
Teleconferencing, 220
Telephone directories ads in, 62
Telephone (Audio Conferencing), 220
Television
- coming of, 17
- advantage to advertisers, 60
- sex in, 90
- importance as a medium, 90-92
Ten Memorable Ad Campaigns, 28
Testimonials, 65

TV Codes, 95, 97
TV Commercials, 60
- time limits, 60

TV in India history, 168
TV programmes
- types, 93
- Signs used, 93
- stereotypes, 93
- understanding, 96
- sex in, 97

TV viewership status, 171
Touch and Feel Merchandise, 167
Traditional Media
- advantages, 143
- disadvantages, 143
- importance, 143
- companies using, 144
- types used in villages, 144

Transportation signs, 61
Tuff shoes ad, 49

U

Unethical Ads, 50
Upward Communication, 216
Users' Rights internet advertising, 44

Villagers as buyers, 151

V

Voice Mail (Audio Conferencing), 220
Vulgarity in Ads, 133

W

Ways of advertising, 57, 61
Wall paintings, 149
Window displays, 61
Window dressing, 166
Women's
- status in India, 101
- portrayal in magazines, 101, 132
- emergence as consumers, 102

Women's Magazines in India, 103
- advertising in, 103

Women's Sexuality, 83
Written Communication, 197, 221
- types, 198
- advantages, 198